CW01667569

VAN GOGH STUDIES

FIVE CRITICAL ESSAYS

JOHN A. WALKER

JAW publications

87 Hillfield Ave, London N8 7DG

For Sophie

1981

Designed by Katherine Tattersall

International Standard Book Number: 0 9507486 0 9

Cover illus, *Landscape with a hut in the Camargue* (detail) Arles 1888, pen and ink, 34.5 x 25.5 cm, Amsterdam, Rijksmuseum Vincent van Gogh.

CONTENTS

Bibliographical note

'Van Gogh's colour theories' was first written in 1960-62 as a thesis for a degree at Kings College, Newcastle-Upon-Tyne, Durham University; a revised version is presented here. 'The van Gogh industry' was first published in *Art and Artists* 11 (5) August 1976; 'Van Gogh as a peasant painter' in *Artery* (17) December 1979; and 'Art history versus philosophy' in *Block* (2) Spring 1980.

INTRODUCTION

This book consists of five studies of the work of Vincent van Gogh written at intervals during a twenty year period. In the introduction I would like to explain, briefly, how my interest in van Gogh's work was aroused, and to indicate the rationale underlying each of the studies. The essays are presented in the order in which they were written because in this way changes of approach and emphasis in the intellectual project through time become evident.

Although I am employed as an art historian in institutions of higher education, I am not a van Gogh scholar in the sense of being a specialist in his oeuvre. Van Gogh is a subject to which I have returned periodically; on each occasion I have assumed that this would be the last time I would write about him, but each time circumstances have shown this to be a premature assumption. When writing the essays in this book the kind of readers I had in mind were art students and the general public rather than my fellow art historians.

Today we live in an environment which is exceptionally rich in visual imagery – I am thinking in particular of the huge, full-colour advertising hoardings which are such a common feature of the urban landscape, of colour supplements, of colour television, and of the displays of glossy magazines to be found in most newsagents. In sharp contrast, the period in which I grew up – the period of the second world war and the years of austerity which followed it – was notable for the absence of such visual stimuli. Admittedly there were pictorial magazines such as *Picture Post* and *Everybody's,* twice weekly visits to the cinema, and children's comics, but even so the environment was remarkably bare compared to the situation now. The provincial town of my youth – Grimsby, Lincolnshire – lacked a municipal art gallery, consequently despite an early interest in drawing and painting I had virtually no first hand experience of original paintings and sculptures until my teens. Even reproductions were scarce: the town was without a good modern bookshop; the only new art books around appeared in the main newsagent's shop. At that time the kind of shops, which are now commonplace, devoted to the sale of prints, posters and postcards did not exist. The local library was for me a primary source of intellectual stimulation during my childhood and adolescence, but its stock of art books was extremely limited and many fewer art books were being published then than is the case now. The only art periodical in evidence was *The Studio,* at that time a depressing production whose theoretical/intellectual level was extremely low.

Not only was the external environment lacking in visual imagery, so were the internal spaces: the working class home in which I lived had no paintings or reproductions on the walls; nor at first did the schools I attended. It is for these reasons that I recall with great vividness the arrival in the early 1950s in the art room of the grammar school of six large-scale reproductions of oil paintings (circulated by the Arts Council?). In every art lesson my gaze was drawn irresistably to these images. It is obvious to me now that they fulfilled a lack of which I had, until that point in time, been unaware. Of the six images I remember particularly Bruegel's 'Winter landscape', Renoir's 'Les parapluies', a view of a town square with a statue by Raoul Dufy, and one of van Gogh's 'Sunflowers' series. This is my first recollection of any contact with the art of van Gogh – I was aged twelve or thirteen at the time. I can remember being puzzled and intrigued by the fact that most of the colours used where shades of yellow. This seemed to contradict an aesthetic rule I was already conscious of: 'always seek a contrast of colours, never paint a picture in just one colour'. The artist's drawing and handling also seemed extraordinarily crude and 'primitive' compared to the degree of finish I was seeking to achieve in my own water colours.

A few years later I was to have a further contact with van Gogh's work which was to be much more decisive. As I have already explained, there was no art gallery in the town, public or private, consequently we never saw any visiting exhibitions. In the winter of 1955-56 a large-scale exhibition of van Gogh's paintings and drawings was shown at Liverpool, Manchester and Newcastle-upon-Tyne. My art teacher, Ernest Worrall, organized a coach trip from Grimsby to Manchester one chilly day to see this exhibition. The trip was for adults only – members of a local Art Society, I think – but I managed to get a seat. I was seventeen years old. This was my first exposure to a large-scale exhibition of modern, original oil paintings and drawings. Its impact upon me was tremendous: I found the work powerful, overwhelming, exhilerating. For the first time I appreciated what original art of the highest level was like; what an extraordinary psychological impact – emotional, aesthetic – art could make. I had already determined to be a painter but this exhibition confirmed the correctness of my choice of vocation.

On my return from Manchester I immediately began reading about van Gogh's life and work, my interest having been aroused by the fragments of information gleaned from the catalogue, my teacher's comments, and from the images themselves. I began by reading non-critical, biographical accounts such as L. & E. Hanson's *Portrait of Vincent* (Chatto & Windus, 1955), and then gravitated to better texts such as Carl Nordenfalk's *The life and work of van Gogh* (Elek, 1953) (which I still regard as an excellent introduction). Later at Durham University where I studied Fine Art, I bought Vincent's complete letters in three volumes when they were published in England in 1958. Towards my degree I wrote a thesis on van Gogh's colour theories. Some years later I made a pilgrimage to Arles to study his Provençal motifs at first hand. The initial impact of van Gogh's life and work had been strongly emotional but I quickly developed a distaste for the way in which in the literature on him the subjective dimension was stressed at the expense of the objective, the spontaneous at the expense of the planned, the irrational at the expense of the rational, the insane at the expense of the sane. The more I studied it, the more it seemed to me that Vincent's work was eminently lucid and sane, despite the more melodramatic incidents in his life. And I discovered from his letters that he was a learned, cultivated, thoughtful individual, that he was an artist who was fully conversant with the art theory of his day and who consciously planned his compositions and colour schemes. All the work I have done on van Gogh has been motivated by the desire to do justice to the rational and humanitarian being as against the wild, tortured genius which plays such a central role in the van Gogh myth.

Essay two, concerning Provence and van Gogh's motifs, was prompted by a desire to see at first hand the physical environment in which van Gogh lived for a short but remarkably productive period. I wrote it after spending a fortnight's holiday in Provence in the early 1960s. (At the time I worked for Camden Public Libraries and the text was used to accompany a small display of books and photographs on the theme of van Gogh's Provençal motifs). Ernst Gombrich's *Art and illusion,* first published in 1960, made a deep impression upon me. His discussion of the psychology of pictorial representation seemed very important to my practice as a painter. The book also raised the whole problem of the relationship between art and reality, between pictures and their referents. Before I went to the South of France I only knew Provence from van Gogh's paintings and drawings, and from photographs. Seeing it directly made me realize the marked difference between past and present, between a motif and its pictorial representation, and the considerable differences between the representation of a motif in the medium of oil painting and in the rival medium of photography.

By the mid 1970s, when I wrote *'The van Gogh industry',* I had produced two books on contemporary art and several pieces of art criticism. My knowledge of the social and economic context within which art and criticism are generated had expanded greatly from my student days. During the early 1970s I also acquired a political consciousness which I had not possessed before. Disenchantment with the way in which art was exploited by dealers, collectors, scholars, critics and the mass media inspired the third essay. At that point I had no intention of writing on van Gogh again because I naturally wanted to avoid contributing to the very 'industry' which I was criticizing. However, further contributions were necessitated by what I came to regard as inadequate accounts and misreadings of his work.

'Van Gogh as a peasant painter', the fourth essay, was originally written in the late 1970s as a chapter in a book on the topic of Art and the Peasantry (this book has not been published). At that time the peasantry was a subject which had become very fashionable amongst certain intellectuals through exhibitions of the work of Courbet and Millet, through the writings of Teodor Shanin and John Berger, through the work of various European film-makers, and through a growing consciousness in the city dwellers of the advanced industrial countries of the plight of the peasantry in the Third World, and the problems being experienced by peasants employed as guest workers in European factories. My interest in the peasantry was, I freely acknowledge, prompted by these cultural influences. Of particular concern to me was the way in which peasants, manual labour, and the country/city relationship had been depicted in the art of the past. The issue of representation was pertinent because it had a bearing upon the manner in which workers are to be depicted by socialist artists today, and by the way men and women are to be represented by feminist artists and film-makers.

The final and most recent essay – *'Art history versus philosophy'* – written in the early 1980s, was prompted by two factors: firstly, a series of articles by different writers concerning the meaning of a van Gogh painting which seemed to me inadequate in their conclusions; and secondly, a growing interest in the theoretical and historiographical problems of art history as a discipline. The essay emerged as an offshoot of a much larger project, namely a theoretical study of art history which attempts to update the discipline by taking account of twentieth century advances in Marxism, linguistics, semiotics and film theory.

As already explained, each time I completed an essay on van Gogh I imagined that there was nothing more to be said, that his work had been exhausted of its meaning and significance, but each time I have had to revise my views; the work of art history/criticism, it would appear, is never finally concluded.

VAN GOGH'S COLOUR THEORIES

AND THEIR RELEVANCE TO THE PAINTINGS OF THE ARLES PERIOD

Introduction

Van Gogh's early paintings – those of the Dutch period – are sombre in colouration and pessimistic in feeling; his later paintings – in particular those of the Arles period – are lighter in tone, brighter in colour, and, in the main, more optimistic in sentiment. The two periods can be characterized in terms of a transition from dark to light, from tone to colour. Nevertheless, a chronological examination of the evolution of van Gogh's ideas about colour will demonstrate the continuity of his thought, and will show that the foundations for the colour theory informing his mature work were laid during the period spent in Holland.

The following essay is divided into three parts: Part I traces the development of his ideas on colour from July 1882 to November 1885; Part II describes, briefly, the impact of Antwerp and Paris on his colour theory; Part III reviews van Gogh's reasons for moving to Provence and examines various applications of his colour theories in representative paintings.

Some psychologists have seen van Gogh's passion for colour as a symptom of his mental aberration; this is a problem I have not attempted to address in this essay.

Part I : July 1882 – November 1885

Before discussing van Gogh's early work, some of the difficulties involved in painting the visible world need to be mentioned. When novices begin to paint they often assume that a convincing pictorial likeness of the world can be achieved by a copying process in which the local colours of objects are matched by the colours mixed on the palette. 'Local' colours are those which appear to belong naturally to objects, for example, the green of grass, the red of post boxes, etc. In fact, the colour of an object varies according to a number of factors: different types of illumination; by what colours surround it; the distance of the observer from the object; and so forth. Beginners also discover that even in the controlled conditions of a studio it is exceedingly difficult to match the colours of objects by mixtures of pigments. It is especially difficult to render in paint an object such as stained glass whose colour is the result of light illuminating it from within. The brightness of light sources such as the sun or lamps cannot be matched by a pigment, even a pure white. Once beginners realize the problems of painting from Nature – though few formulate them consciously – they cast around for alternative methods of depicting the world besides that of copying/matching local colours.

Two years after beginning to draw in the Borinage, van Gogh began to paint in oils.[1] He was at once confronted by the problem of colour. Theo was soon informed of van Gogh's first opinion on the matter, which was that there were scarcely any colours which were not shades of grey. It seems probable that Theo questioned his brother's remark and gave the Impressionist view that there is no black in Nature, for in his next letter to Theo Vincent observed:

"As I understand it we of course agree completely about black in Nature. Absolute black does not really exist . . . there are only three fundamental colours red, yellow and blue; 'composites' are orange, green and purple. By adding black and some white one gets the endless varieties of greys . . . the whole chemistry of colours is not more complicated than those simple rules . . . the colourist is the man who knows how to find Nature's greys on his palette".[2]

The emphasis upon the use of grey is the result of the lingering impression of tuition in oils and water-colour given to van Gogh by his cousin Anton Mauve in December 1881. It is perhaps significant that van Gogh refers to colour as a 'chemistry' because it demonstrates his willingness to seek scientific, rational reasons to justify his practice as a painter. Later he was to cite 'the laws' of colour.[3] From his concluding definition it is clear that in 1882 van Gogh did not think of a colourist as a person who invented or improvised colour schemes but as one who sought to render the local colours of the natural world as faithfully as possible. This was the conventional, academic conception of a colourist in Holland during the second half of the nineteenth century.

While painting his early studies van Gogh became aware that certain colour combinations – harmonious or contrasting – possessed a quality of inevitability. This experience is shared by so many that it necessitates a physiological explanation. Though van Gogh found painting *"a strong means of expression"*, yet *"at the same time one can express tender things with it too, let a soft grey or green speak amid all the ruggedness"*. It is significant that van Gogh, from the very outset, thinks of colour relationships as being capable of communicating emotions. Another remark concerning his aims as a painter – *"to make it as I see it before I set to work to make it as I feel it"*[4] – indicates the priority which van Gogh assigned to visible reality. Van Gogh, like Courbet, adopted an empirical approach to painting. Emotion was extremely important to van Gogh but it had to be reached through appearances, through the representation of the contemporary world. The objective came before the subjective.

In one of his descriptions to Theo of his experiences before the motif, van Gogh observed how brilliant the green of young beech trees appeared against a background of reddish-brown. Here, van Gogh is noticing the mutual enhancement of complementary colours – red and green – caused by the optical phenomenon known as simultaneous contrast.[5]

It was another two years after writing of his colour system based upon the three fundamental hues red, yellow and blue, that van Gogh's attention was again directed to the problem of colour theory. His renewed interest was prompted largely by the technical and historical art books which he read between August 1884 and November 1885.[6] Van Gogh was particularly impressed by Charles Blanc's *Les artistes de mon temps.* He quoted Blanc's opinion – that great colourists are those who do not paint local colour – to Theo and explained how this opinion had been confirmed by Delacroix who in turn had cited Veronese as an example of an artist who could paint the blond-coloured flesh of a nude with the dirty tone of the pavement. Under the influence of such eminent authorities, van Gogh began to question the academic canon of Mauve: *"I am not quite convinced yet that a grey sky, for instance, must always be painted in the local tone"*, when equally, *"one can express light by opposing it to black"*.[7] Van Gogh was beginning to realize that it is fallacy to suppose that the optical experience of Nature can be rendered accurately in painting by the method of matching the local colours of objects, because this is to assume that each local colour or tone exists independently of its neighbouring tones and colours. (Perhaps the only conceivable way of painting with this aim in mind would be to isolate each tone by (a) peering down a cardboard tube of some kind; or (b), by taking the canvas off the easel and comparing each tone in the motif with its corresponding tone on the canvas.) The conclusion which van Gogh was to draw from such musings was identical to that reached by the Impressionists and Pointillists, namely, that to render local colour was an impossible task, that each colour had to be related to every other colour on the canvas and not to those which appeared in the motif. As van Gogh himself put it:

"Suppose I have to paint an autumn landscape, trees with yellow leaves . . . when I conceive it as a symphony in yellow, what does it matter if the fundamental colour of yellow is the same as that of the leaves or not? It matters very ***little****; everything depends on my perception of the infinite variety of tones of the same* ***family****"*.[8]

In other words, all that is required to achieve a convincing illusion of reality is not perfect one-to-one correspondance between the local colours of objects and their pictorial representations, but a scale or gradient of colour or tone equivalent to that of Nature. Having grasped this principle, van Gogh was able to become progressively more 'arbitrary' in his use of colour.

A month before he left Nuenen for Antwerp, van Gogh succinctly explained the minor revolution his art had undergone: *"One starts with a hopeless struggle to follow Nature and everything goes wrong; one ends by calmly creating from one's palette and Nature agrees with it and follows."*[9]

Impressed by the quality of Blanc's ideas, van Gogh acquired another book by him – *Grammaire des arts et dessin* – which contains a chapter devoted to colour which van Gogh summarized for Theo. Blanc's knowledge of colour was based on conversations with Delacroix, close study of the works of Rubens and Velasquez in the Louvre, and the discoveries of the scientists Sutter, Helmholtz,Rood, and especially Chevreul, the man who had formulated the law of simulataneous contrast in 1839. The primary colours named by Blanc – red, yellow and blue – ultimately derived from Thomas Young who expounded a three-colour theory in 1801, accorded with those of van Gogh, as did the secondaries – orange, green and violet (these correspond to van Gogh's 'composities'). The painter's observation of the green-red contrast between the beech trees and their background found theoretical confirmation in the law of simultaneous contrast, and his feeling that certain colour combinations were 'inevitable' found objective support in the account of complementary colours (which are a special case, and which provide the most vivid examples of, the law of simultaneous contrast). Van Gogh also reviewed the effects of mixing colours, of various types of juxtapositions, harmonic combinations, and altering hues merely by changing their contexts.

There only remained one colour phenomenon cited by Blanc which van Gogh had not observed by himself. This was the optical mixture of small patches of colour that occurs when they are viewed from a sufficient distance. Blanc mentioned this effect and with this spur van Gogh noticed immediately that the plaids woven by the peasants of Nuenen, although multicoloured, appeared harmonious at a distance. With this item of knowledge he became fully acquainted with the concerns of the Neo-Impressionists before he had seen one of their paintings. However, this knowledge did not result in a method or technique which in any way resembled their's (not surprisingly, because at this time van Gogh had only a hazy notion of what an Impressionist painting looked like.) He did modify his technique, but in the direction of chiaroscuro. At first sight this appears to have been a backward step, but it seemed the only alternative to the by now despised task of seizing local colours. Van Gogh's efforts to reconcile, by means of chiaroscuro, the needs of form and solidity with the theories of pure colour resulted in *"a kind of gymnastics"*.[10] His admiration was torn between the work of those he called 'harmonists' – Millet, Rembrandt, Israels – and the work of those he called 'colourists' – Hals, Veronese, Rubens, Velasquez and Delacroix. The way in which his 'gymnastics' were resolved is the subject of an article by Carlo Derkert which describes how the dark tones of his chiaroscuro modelling were produced by mixtures of complementary colours instead of the traditional combination of local colours and black.[11] The colouration of such works as *'The potatoe eaters', 'The Bible and the French novel', 'Four bird's nests'* and the series of *'Peasants' heads'* shows evidence of van Gogh's new method of mixing pigments. In these canvases, definite complementary colour juxtapositions can be detected, even though they are very muted compared to those which were to follow. It was these early, tentative experiments which paved the way for the intense complementary colour combinations independent of tonal graduations typical of the Arles period.

A pictorial theme which has been traditional in Western European art for many centuries is that of the four seasons. These are generally represented in terms of the various kinds of crops, weather, and labours undertaken by peasants, typical of the different phases of the year. In 1884, van Gogh produced a series of sketches for paintings on the theme of the seasons. Each season, van Gogh considered, could best be represented by means of a dominant colour combination: Spring by red and green; Summer by blue and orange; Autumn by yellow and violet; and Winter by white and black. These colour pairs had some objective justification, for example, the red and green of Spring were suggested to van Gogh by the green of young corn and the pink of apple blossom. Descriptions of the seasons series in his letters exhibit the by now familiar progression which van Gogh made from the observed object to a simplified colour combination, which in turn signifies an emotion or abstract conception, in this case the different moods of the seasons.

A theoretical issue arising from the above may be stated as follows: van Gogh sought to employ combinations of complementary colours in order to communicate to others certain emotions and ideas, but to what extent were these specific to van Gogh, that is, personal to him, and to what extent were they conventional, that is, common to a cultural community? Do we have to learn a private code or 'language' to grasp the meaning of a van Gogh painting or can we 'read' his pictures fairly easily because we already understand the code or 'language' in which his pictorial statements are couched?

At this point it is appropriate to consider another facet of van Gogh's interest in colour, that is, his use of the analogy with music. In January 1883 van Gogh found that the techniques of various artists reminded him of the sounds of musical instruments, for example, Lemud, Daumier, and Lançon reminded him of the sound of a violin, Garvarni and Bodmer were like the sound of a piano and Millet was akin to the sound of a stately organ. Later, in July 1884, he found in the colour of Dupré *"something of a splendid symphony"*[12] reminiscent of the music of Beethoven. These observations were confirmed by Charles Blanc who believed painting to be between music and sculpture, that colour could be taught in a systematic way like music, and that it was easier to learn than drawing. Blanc explained Newton's conclusion that there were seven colours in the spectrum as a proposition designed to find a poetical analogy with the seven notes of music. A passage from Euler was also quoted by Blanc to the effect that there was a perfect parallel between light and sound, between the senses of sight and hearing, because both depended upon similar vibrations. Stimulated by these speculative remarks, van Gogh took lessons from an old music teacher. A friend of van Gogh's – Anton Kerssemakers – recalls that during these lessons Vincent continually compared the notes of the piano with a range of colours. The music teacher thought he had to do with a madman and discontinued the lessons.

Expressions like 'notes of colours', 'colour harmonies', and 'orchestrations of colour' are commonly used by painters in connection with their art,and the habit of comparing music and painting can be traced back at least as far as Aristotle. Parallels between the two arts were, however, treated in an exceptionally literal manner in the second half of the nineteenth century. Baudelaire discussed the correspondances between music and painting, and Monet, Signac and Whistler gave musical titles to their works. According to James Laver, the musical titles of Whistler *"served to remind the artist himself of the need for simplicity and the peril of subordinating general effect to local colour: and it served to remind the public that whatever else he was trying to do he was not attempting to tell a story"*.[13] Similarly, in van Gogh's case the abstract qualities of music provided a useful standard of comparison with which to justify his art against the dogmas of the academicians and the commercialism of art firms such as Goupils.

To stress the 'musicality' (or the 'poetic character') of a painting is to call attention to its formal and syntactic structure, the fact that it consists of a series of interrelated elements which are capable of generating emotional and aesthetic effects independently of content or subject matter.

Music is often cited by painters as an ideal to which painting should aspire because they consider it, simplistically, as a completely abstract art. Yet none of the nineteenth century artists who made use of the analogy with music were advocating total abstraction: figuration was still essential to their conception of art; this was especially true in van Gogh's case. In his work colour may constantly strive to float free of objective reference but it is always in the end anchored to an image by muscular brush drawing and thick pigment.

Part II : Antwerp and Paris, November 1885 – February 1888

Van Gogh once expressed the opinion that an understanding of the laws of colour enabled one to graduate from an instinctive belief in the great masters to an analysis of why one admired them. In Antwerp he visited the city museum to study works by Rembrandt, Hals and Rubens. He was especially impressed by a portrait by Rubens. With the help of a colour manufacturer called Tyck he succeeded in analysing Rubens' colour technique and, encouraged by its frankness, he used brighter colour in his own work and extended his palette to include carmine, cadmium yellow, and viridian green. Furthermore, van Gogh found that Rubens expressed moods of cheerfulness, serenity and sorrow via colour combinations. Increasingly van Gogh sought to communicate a single emotion, or set of closely related emotions, per painting. For example, in a portrait of a female dancer painted in Antwerp he said he wanted to express something "*voluptuous and at the same time cruelly tormented*".[14]

While in Antwerp van Gogh attended the local academy of art; he also frequented student drawing clubs. The disputes between van Gogh and his tutors at the academy concerning the methods and goals of drawing are well known but colour does not seem to have been discussed to the same degree. The only remark dealing with colour theory at the academy is a comment by van Gogh on the paintings of the staff to the effect that they showed no understanding or appreciation of colour. Evidently van Gogh thought the academy had nothing to teach him on this score.

Van Gogh's solitary meditations on the nature of art and colour were the subject of everyday debate amongst the avant garde artists of Paris. His contacts with the principal figures of the day have been fully documented, as have his achievements in mastering the techniques of Impressionism and Pointillism. It is necessary, however, to try to resolve certain ambivalences in van Gogh's attitude to the various influences to which he was subjected in Paris.

It is not generally realised that van Gogh was disappointed with the first Impressionist exhibition which he visited, largely because it was unrepresentative of the major figures of the movement. Only through working in the open air and by gaining a close acquaintance with the paintings of Monet, which he saw at Durand-Ruel's, did he come to respect Impressionism. The swift succession of events during those hectic years made Impressionism outmoded by 1886. One would have supposed that van Gogh's interest in colour theory would have led him to embrace Pointillism – then at its peak – wholeheartedly, but he called its technique 'stippling' showing that he regarded it as a method of enlivening the picture surface rather than as a complete aesthetic system. No doubt van Gogh's empiricism and impetuosity made a total conversion impossible, nevertheless, A.S. Hartrick has testified to van Gogh's thorough knowledge of Seurat's theories: "*he (van Gogh) was particularly pleased with a theory that the eye carried a portion of the last sensation it had enjoyed into the next so that something of both must be included in every picture made*".[15] And at Arles, as we shall see, van Gogh was to make use of this and other of Seurat's ideas and pictorial devices.

Although van Gogh expressed disdain for the Baudelairian aspect of Paris, the Symbolist movement had a significant influence upon him. Many of its ideas coincided with his own, and his friends Gauguin, Signac and Bernard were enthusiastic about the musicality of painting and the emotional qualities of colours. They all shared the Symbolist writers' admiration of Wagner and sought to compare such artists as Puvis de Chavannes, Degas, Cézanne and Monet to the composer. Van Gogh wrote to his first critic Aurier from St Rémy of his reluctance to be cast in the role of a Symbolist, and later he remarked to Theo that he would rather be a "*shoemaker than a musician in colours*".[16] He feared that the literary bias of Symbolism would distract him from what he called "*the possible, the logical, the real*".[17] Despite these anti-Symbolist sentiments, the ideas of the movement left their mark, particularly in relation to the suggestive power of colour.

In order to develop his mastery of colour van Gogh painted, in Paris, a whole series of studies of flowers: "*Red poppies, blue cornflowers and myosotys, white and rose roses, yellow chrysanthemums – seeking oppositions of blue with orange, red and green, yellow and violet seeking* ***les tons rompus et neutres*** *to harmonize brutal extremes. Trying to render intense colour and not a grey harmony*".[18] Like Delacroix, van Gogh carried in his pockets balls of coloured wool and chalks with which to experiment when an idea struck him.

It is clear that the fundamental characteristics of van Gogh's art – his empiricism, his emotional response to colour, his penchant for a scientific system of colour – were established in Holland, despite the fact that the paintings of the Dutch period do not obviously demonstrate this. Though his mind was prepared his hand needed the practice afforded by Antwerp and Paris; his eye needed the example of the lighter palette of the Impressionists, and the vivid colour schemes of the Neo-Impressionists and Symbolists, plus the stimulus of the almost tropical light of Provence.

Part III : The South; the paintings of the Arles period

Daudet's descriptions of sun and the effects of light in Tarascon whetted van Gogh's appetite for the South. Delacroix, he recalled, had gone all the way to Africa in search of simultaneous contrasts;

and Monticelli in Marseilles had discarded "*local truth*"[19] for the richness of colour. Van Gogh considered that he was continuing the tradition established by Veronese, Titian, Velasquez and Goya, and in regard to colour he felt better theoretically equipped than they because of the knowledge he possessed of "*the prism and its properties*".[20] Thus his journey to Arles was a rationalization of his desire for dramatic contrasts of colour.

In itself the climatic difference between Holland and Provence is not sufficient to explain the radical change in his work between the Dutch and Arles periods. The dark colouring of the early works was as much a reflection of van Gogh's attitude to life, at that time, as to the dull skies and poor lighting in the peasant huts of the North. The vividness of van Gogh's colour was always proportional to his personal confidence: after the fracas with Gauguin he slipped automatically into muted, naturalistic colour which lasted until his confidence had been restored. A similar change is discernible between the Provençal and the Auvers pictures. No doubt van Gogh found northern France less colourful than Provence but a more significant factor was his increasing despair regarding his mental condition and uncertainty about his source of finance; these worries restricted the inventiveness of his palette.

Clearly, the South is not as van Gogh painted it. Signac for one found it luminous rather than colourful. Both artists were conditioned by their respective colour theories; van Gogh sought, in the main, large areas of colour, while Signac, the avowed Pointillist, was concerned with reflections and the breakdown of local colours into their constituents.

It is impossible to describe in detail all the Arles paintings – almost two hundred works – therefore various examples have been selected to illustrate van Gogh's use of colour.

In many of the works of the Arles period van Gogh rendered colour naturalistically, that is, he used local colours as a starting point. However, comparisons with the motifs shows that he simplified and intensified the colours which he found in Nature. Furthermore, he included colours caused by the optical system of the observer. For example, in the painting '*The village of Saintes-Maries*' there are houses with bright orange roofs and walls of a strong violet-blue. The local colour of the walls was grey or white not violet-blue, consequently the violet-blue is the result of induction caused by the orange of the roofs. The precedent for painting shadows blue was established, of course, by the Impressionists; their pictorial revolution involved a destruction of the constancies of form and colour upon which academic art was based. Van Gogh did not merely tint shadows blue he painted them solidly blue. This is an instance of what van Gogh himself described as 'exaggerated' colour. Exaggerated colour is realistic in the sense that caricatures are realistic: where emphasis results in a more convincing likeness; such was van Gogh's intention: "*Using ... colour as a means of arriving at the expression and intensification of character*".[21]

Not only was van Gogh prepared to heighten the intensity of the colours which he found in Nature, he was also prepared to introduce colours which were not to be found in the motif. For example, he used even the non-pictorial element of his signature 'Vincent' in order to complete a complementary contrast, as in his painting '*The sea at Saintes-Maries*' of which he wrote: "*On one marine there is an excessively red signature because I wanted a red note in the green*".[22]

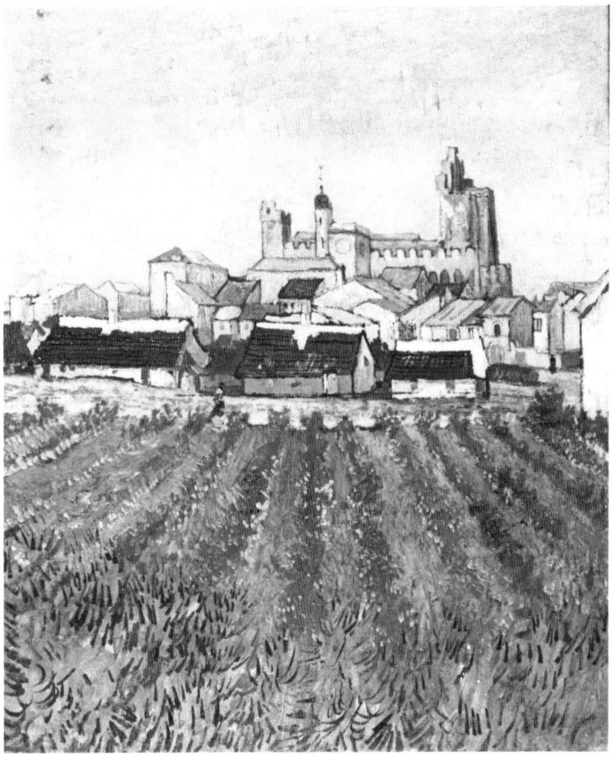

(1) *View of Saintes Maries,* Arles 1888, oil on canvas, 64 x 53 cm, Otterlo, Rijksmuseum Kröller-Müller.

Van Gogh was fully conscious of his deviations from Nature and described his colour as becoming "*more arbitrary*",[23] but clearly at no time during the Arles period was colour left to chance, on the contrary his colour was determined by quasi-scientific notions of harmony and composition, what may be called 'aesthetic' colour. The psychologist Anton Ehrenzweig has observed: "*the artist's urge of justifying artistic innovations by external laws is not determined by a genuine scientific interest in observing Nature but by an internal necessity, that is, the necessity of restricting the thing-free form play which broke loose after the destruction of the rational thing-constancies of size, brightness and colour*" *(which occurred in the nineteenth century).*[24]

Van Gogh was rarely content to paint only one version of a motif which interested him. The wooden drawbridges of the Arles canal for example, which attracted him in part because of their resemblance to those of Holland, inspired several works; pictures which show the bridges under different conditions of illumination and from different angles. Other subjects which prompted series were the orchards, the Roulin family, the sower, the reaper, sunflowers, his bedroom, and self-portraits. Van-Gogh's aim in producing series and replicas was to exhaust the motif of its pictorial potential, to experiment with different colour schemes, and to produce a set of works which would serve as decorative schemes: he often envisaged paintings from different series being combined to constitute a decorative scheme in their own right.

Generally speaking, the first painting of a series includes both naturalistic and exaggerated colours; the relationship between the two is sometimes rather uneasy. However, as the series progressed a process of liberation from the object took place as exaggerated and aesthetic colour gained in ascendency. The final painting of a series is invariably distinguished from the first by its more intense colour, by the greater flatness with which the colour is applied, and by simplications in detail and composition. One of the reasons van Gogh gave for using intense colours was his belief that the colours made fashionable by the Impressionists were unstable and, as he expected them to mellow with time, there was "*all the more reason not to be afraid to lay them on too crudely*".[25]

The transition from naturalistic/exaggerated colour to aesthetic colour can be seen clearly in the two '*Self-portraits*' painted immediately after the incident of the ear lobe, which aptly characterize the beginning and end of a typical series. The naturalistic background of the first self-portrait has been replaced in the second by a thing-free harmony of orange and red. The orange being determined by the presence of the blue-voilet hue of van Gogh's hat and the red by the green hue of his coat. A painting from Saint-Rémy – '*Portrait of a servant boy*' – makes use of a similar background, though in this case the colour orange complements a blue smock and the colour red a green hat.

It should be noted that there are certain inconsistencies in van Gogh's naming of the complementaries: at one moment yellow is the complementary of blue, and at another moment it is the complementary of violet. These confusions could not have been resolved without accurate scientific information. In any case van Gogh was not interested in absolute precision; like Delacroix, he did not believe exactitude to be any guarantee of good art. Nevertheless, some kind of rough guidance he found indispensible and so a system of general rules governed his use of complementary contrasts:

Red	green
Blue or violet	yellow or orange

This fourfold schema was employed extensively with minor variations of texture and colour in many of the Arles paintings besides those already cited, for example '*The little Arlésienne*', '*Portrait of Camille Roulin*', '*The Postman*', and '*The Arlésienne*'.

A number of specific decorative devices may also be considered under the heading of aesthetic colour, the first of which is the 'halo',[26] a term used by van Gogh to describe the glow that

(2) *Self-portrait with bandaged ear,* Arles 1889, oil on canvas, 60 x 49 cm, London, Courtauld Institute Galleries.

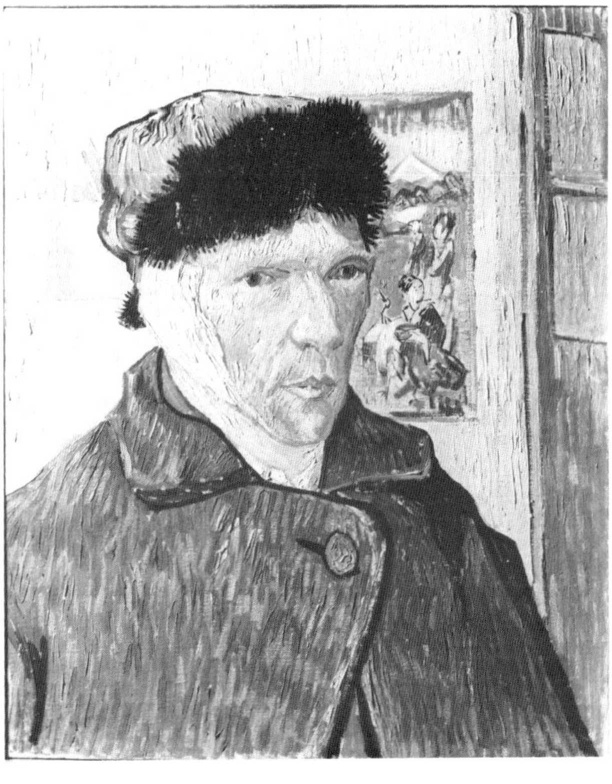

(3) *Self-portrait with bandaged ear and pipe,* Arles 1889, oil on canvas, 51 x 45 cm, Private collection.

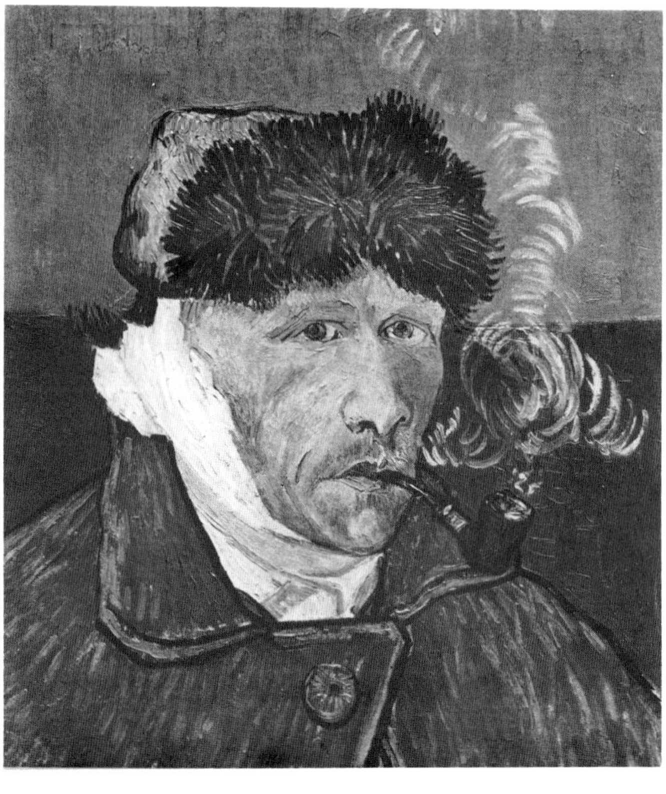

surrounded objects and figures in Pointillist paintings. According to Pointillist theory, the effect of simultaneous contrast was greater at the edges of objects than in their centres, consequently if a Pointillist made a tonal drawing, he or she was required to heighten the white and deepen the black at all points of demarcation in order to enhance the effect; if colour was employed he or she was expected to heighten the contrast by means of complementary colours.

In an article on Cézanne, C. J. R. Frankl describes how a prolonged study of red apples against a grey wall can produce a 'halo'.[27] The red hue of the apples first induces the grey wall to take on a green tinge and this green area will in time shrink, coagulating into a fairly sharply defined rim around the apples of a rather strong green.

Van Gogh knew the work of Seurat intimately. He had seen it in exhibitions and in Seurat's studio. He also knew the paintings of Cézanne which he had seen at Père Tanguy's shop. Several still-lifes of Cézanne from the period in question contain fragmentary statements of the 'halo' phenomenon and it is surely no coincidence that the first example of the 'halo' in van Gogh's oeuvre occurs during his Paris sojourn in the form of a startling red line around the figure of Père Tanguy.

The complexities of the Pointillist aesthetic were schematized by van Gogh into the notion of 'stippling'. Similarly, the 'halo' phenomenon of Neo-Impressionism was schematized into a line of colour. This line or band of colour acted simultaneously as drawing and as colour; generally it was complementary to the colour of the area which it delineated. The line occurs in many of the portraits of the Arles period, in his famous '*Chair*' paintings, and in almost all the still-life paintings but most notably in the sunflower series.

Van Gogh was greatly pleased with a still-life '*A blue enamelled coffee-pot and cup*', a composition in which there are "*six different blues animated by four or five yellows and oranges*".[28] He noticed that when the painting was laid on the red brick floor of his studio in Arles the colours did not become "*hollow or bleached*",[29] as was the case on other backgrounds. In order to retain this adventitious effect, van Gogh painted a border of brilliant red around the edge of the canvas. His precedent for such a border was again the work of Seurat who used colour borders to soften the abrupt transition between the picture and the frame. They appeared in his studies for '*La grande jatte*' as early as 1884, and towards 1888 Seurat began to dot even the frame itself with touches of complementaries in order to bring it into accord with the painting. While van Gogh never indulged in this practice, he did give careful consideration to the colouring of his frames, recommending to Theo the use of Royal blue surrounds for the paintings of the yellow bridges, creamy-white for the orchards, orange frames for the sunflowers, etc. It is a great pity that the directors of public museums and galleries which possess the paintings in question often ignore van Gogh's intentions on this matter.

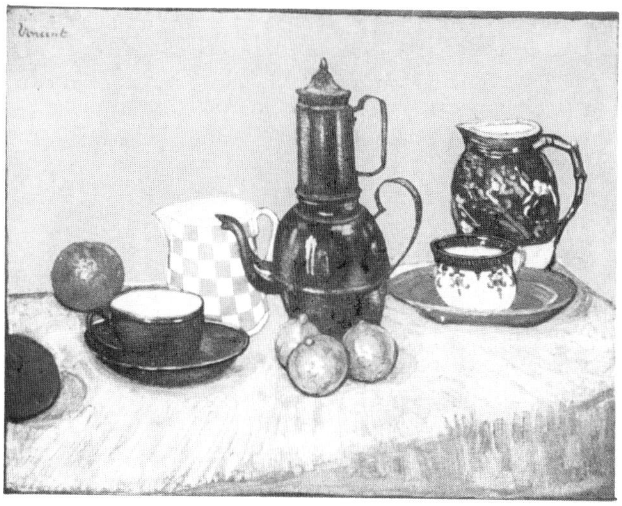

(4) *A blue-enamelled coffee pot and cup,* Arles 1888 oil on canvas, 65 x 81 cm, Lausanne, Goulandris Collection.

The painting '*The house at Arles*' epitomises van Gogh's preoccupation with the blue/yellow contrast. The cobalt hue of the sky, which Roger Fry found "*almost menacing*", is of greater saturation than the yellow of the house and street, but this difference is counter-balanced by the larger surface area of the yellow. The scene reminded van Gogh of the blues and yellows of Vermeer, and by exaggerating all his colours by equal amounts he hoped to achieve a comparable harmony. The initial intensity of the colours – due to the simultaneous contrast between sky and sunlit earth – is increased by the spectator while he or she studies the painting – the result of a further simultaneous contrast induced in his or her eyes by the colours of the painting itself. Thus the spectator participates in the final effect of the work, much as was desired by the Pointillists who expected the public to mix colours optically. That van Gogh was aware of, and deliberately made allowance for, the optical contributions of the viewer seems undeniable in the light of the following comment: "*When one composes a motif of colours ... a yellow evening sky, then the fierce hard white of a white wall against the sky may be expressed ... by raw white softened by a neutral tone, for the sky itself colours it with a delicate lilac hue*".[30]

In Part I certain colour combinations were described as exhibiting a quality of inevitability; the complementary pairs are familiar instances of such combinations. A light mixture of blue and yellow will produce white light: blue reflects predominantly short wavelengths and yellow both long and medium wavelengths, thus covering the range of wavelengths which make up daylight. The human eye, being naturally adjusted to white light, experiences no discomfort before a blue/yellow stimulus. These facts seem to provide a physiological explanation for the feeling of harmony produced by blue/yellow colour combinations such as the one found in van Gogh's painting '*The house at Arles*'.

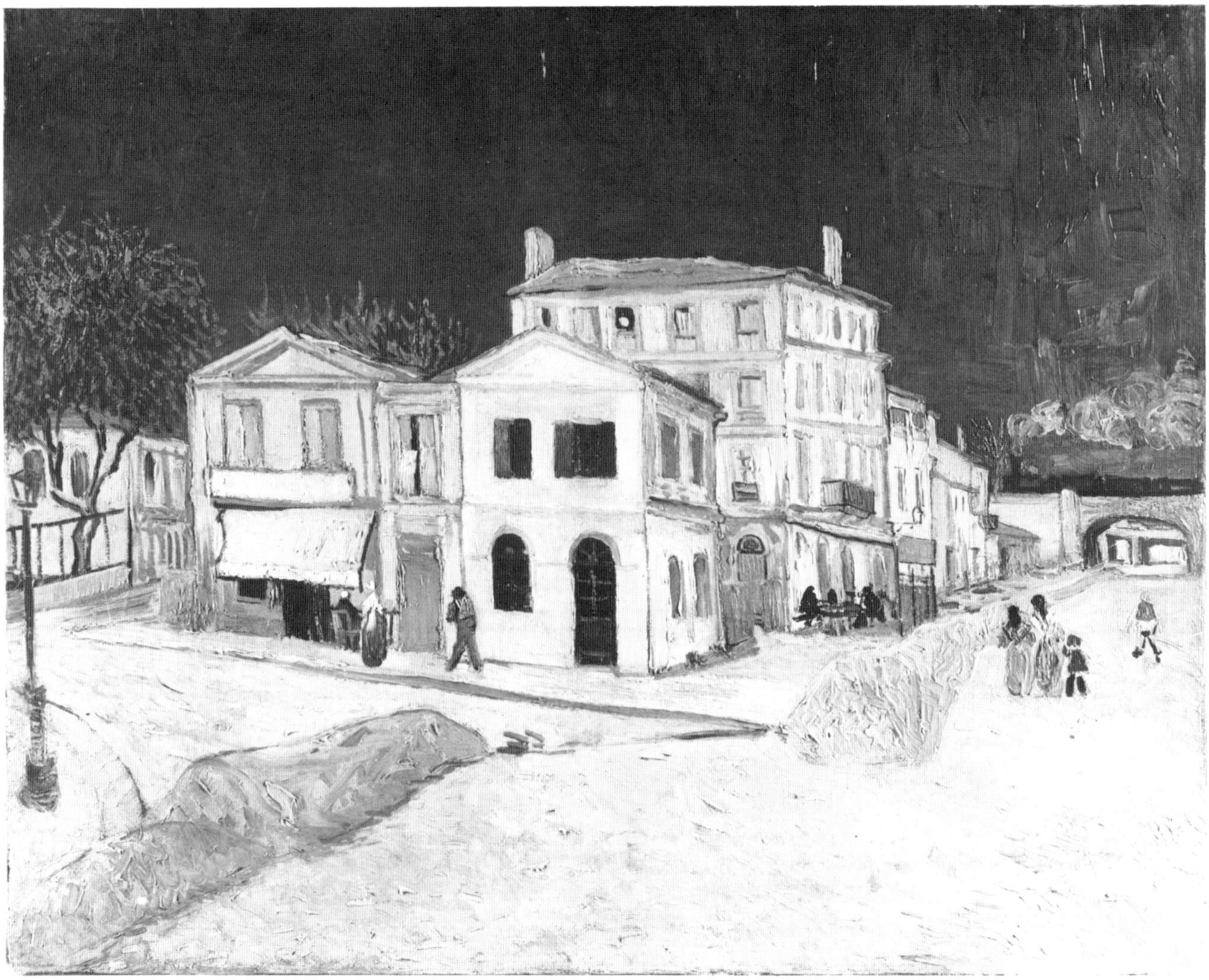

(5) *The yellow house,* Arles 1888, oil on canvas, 76 x 94 cm,Amsterdam, Rijksmuseum Vincent van Gogh.

(6) *Sunflowers,* Arles 1888, oil on canvas, 93 x 73 cm, London, National Gallery.

The above contention is supported by modern psychologists, one of whom writes: "*Experience seems to indicate that the juxtaposition of complementary colours gives rise to an experience of balance and completeness. The stillness of achievement appears as an integration of antagonistic tendencies*".[31] In this instance the opposed tendencies may be listed as follows:

Yellow	*Blue*
Warmth	*Coldness*
Activity	*Passivity*
Nearness (yellow has a high visibility)	*Distance (blue has a low visibility)*
Expansion	*Contraction*
Light	*Dark*

In Arles van Gogh planned a decorative scheme to consist entirely of images of sunflowers. Twelve

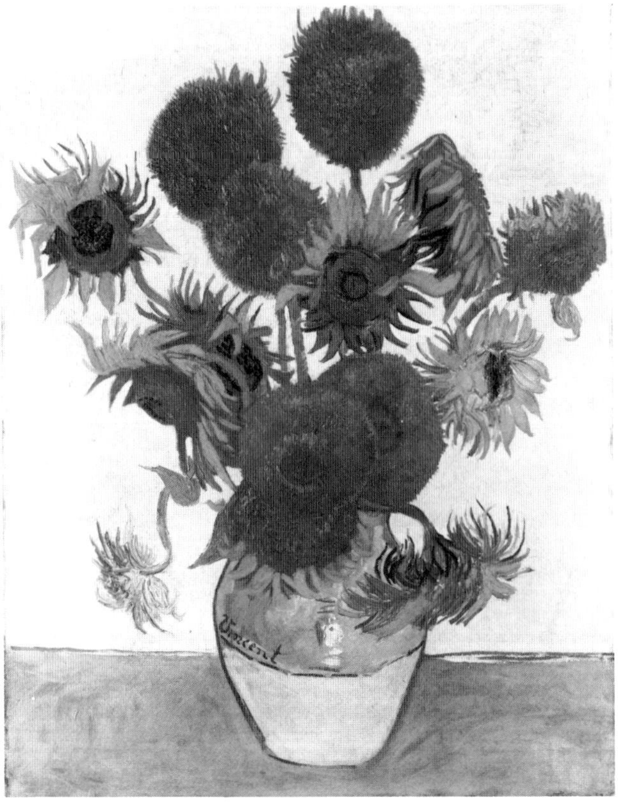

canvases were proposed but only seven actually completed. The sunflower paintings are generally described by critics as *'a harmony of yellows'*, but van Gogh's explicit intention was to create "*a symphony in* ***blue*** *and yellow*"...[32] "*a decoration in which the raw and broken chrome yellows will blaze forth on various grounds – blue from palest malachite green to Royal blue ... effects like those of stained glass windows in a Gothic church*".[33] Blue is virtually absent from the version of the sunflowers in the National Gallery, London, but this does not preclude its influence – at least not in the opinion of one writer: "*the potential energy of the missing complementary vigorously acts on the unconscious mind*".[34] However this may be it is clear from van Gogh's remarks that it would be contrary to his intentions if the sunflower scheme as a whole was judged by just one work, especially a work whose predominant colours are yellow, ochre and green.

At Nuenen, in Holland, van Gogh had described how light can be expressed pictorially by opposing it to black, and later he thought of representing winter by means of a black/white juxtaposition. These two non-colours have one property in common with colours, namely the law of simultaneous contrast. From Arles van Gogh wrote to Emile Bernard of his intention to use black and white pigments straight from the tube in order to rival the effect of Japanese drawings which depend for much of their vividness on the law of contrast. Van Gogh's systematic exploitation of this quality can be seen clearly in his drawing of the stream called *'La Roubine du Roi'*. And this contrast may even be regarded as a colour device: Carl Nordenfalk, commenting on the speckled appearance of van Gogh's drawings, writes: "*the changing character of these patterns conveys an impression of diversity corresponding to the colour impression of a painting. The principle is the same as that of the heraldic method, where the different principle colours are indicated by means of punctuations and line patterns in different directions*".[35]

More speculative ideas for colour schemes to include black and white were communicated to Bernard.[36] Drawings in the letters show that one idea was linked to a motif derived from the village of Saintes-Maries: a white hut with a black door set against orange earth and blue sky; and another from the black-white checked dresses of the Arlésiennes again set against a blue/orange background. Van Gogh's approach to colour was twofold: empirical and at the same time theoretical. In the examples cited above, observation of Nature is of paramount importance, but for the further use of the two non-colours van Gogh turned to a book on colour theory. In *Grammaire des arts et dessin* Blanc had written: "*white and black acting as non-colours will serve to rest the eye, refresh it by moderating the dazzling brilliance of the whole representation*". This was the source of van Gogh's use of white in his painting *'The sower'* which according to him distracts the eye, allowing it to rest "*at the moment when the excessive simultaneous contrast of yellow and violet would irritate it*".[37] A comparable instance of both black and

(7) *La Roubine Du Roi,* Arles 1888, pen and ink, 31.5 x 24 cm. Otterlo, Rijksmuseum Kröller-Müller.

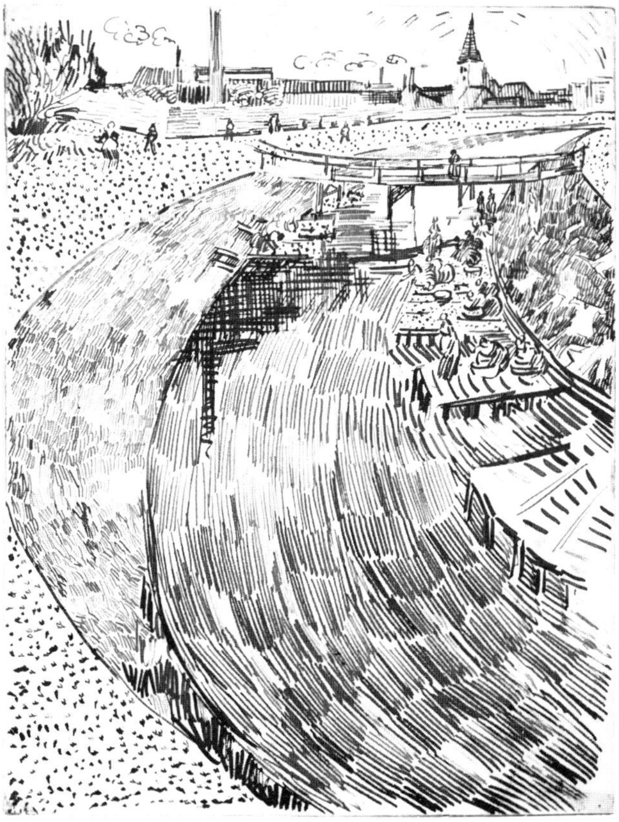

(8) *Two sketches – ideas for colour combinations,* Arles 1888, pen and ink, letter B6 to Emile Bernard.

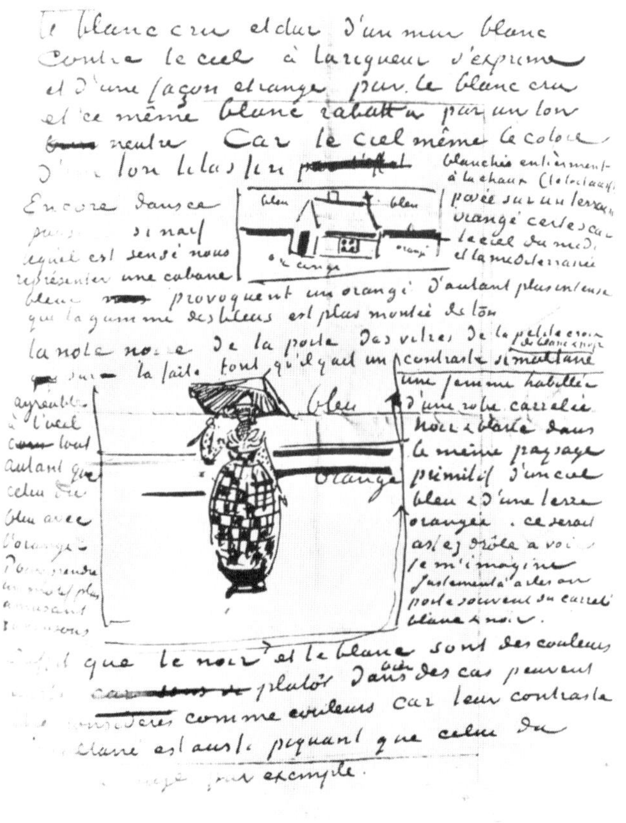
le blanc cru et dur d'un mur blanc
contre le ciel à la rigueur s'exprime
et d'une façon étrange par le blanc cru
et ce même blanc rabattu par un ton
neutre Car le ciel même le colore
d'un ton lilas fin
blanchie entièrement à la chaux (la terrasse) posée sur un terrain orangé certes car le ciel du midi et la méditerranée
Encore dans ce ... si naïf ... qui est censé nous représenter une cabane
bleu ... provoquent un orangé d'autant plus intense que la gamme des bleus est plus montée de ton
la note noire de la porte des vitres de la petite croix ... la faite tout qu'il y ait un contraste simultané
agréable à l'oeil tout autant que celui du bleu avec l'orange
une femme habillée d'une robe carrelée noir et blanc dans le même paysage primitif d'un ciel bleu et d'une terre orangée. ce serait assez drôle à voir je m'imagine justement à Arles on porte souvent du carrelé blanc et noir.
... que le noir et le blanc sont des couleurs ... plutôt dans bien des cas peuvent ... considérés comme couleurs car leur contraste ... blanc est aussi piquant que celui du ... par exemple.

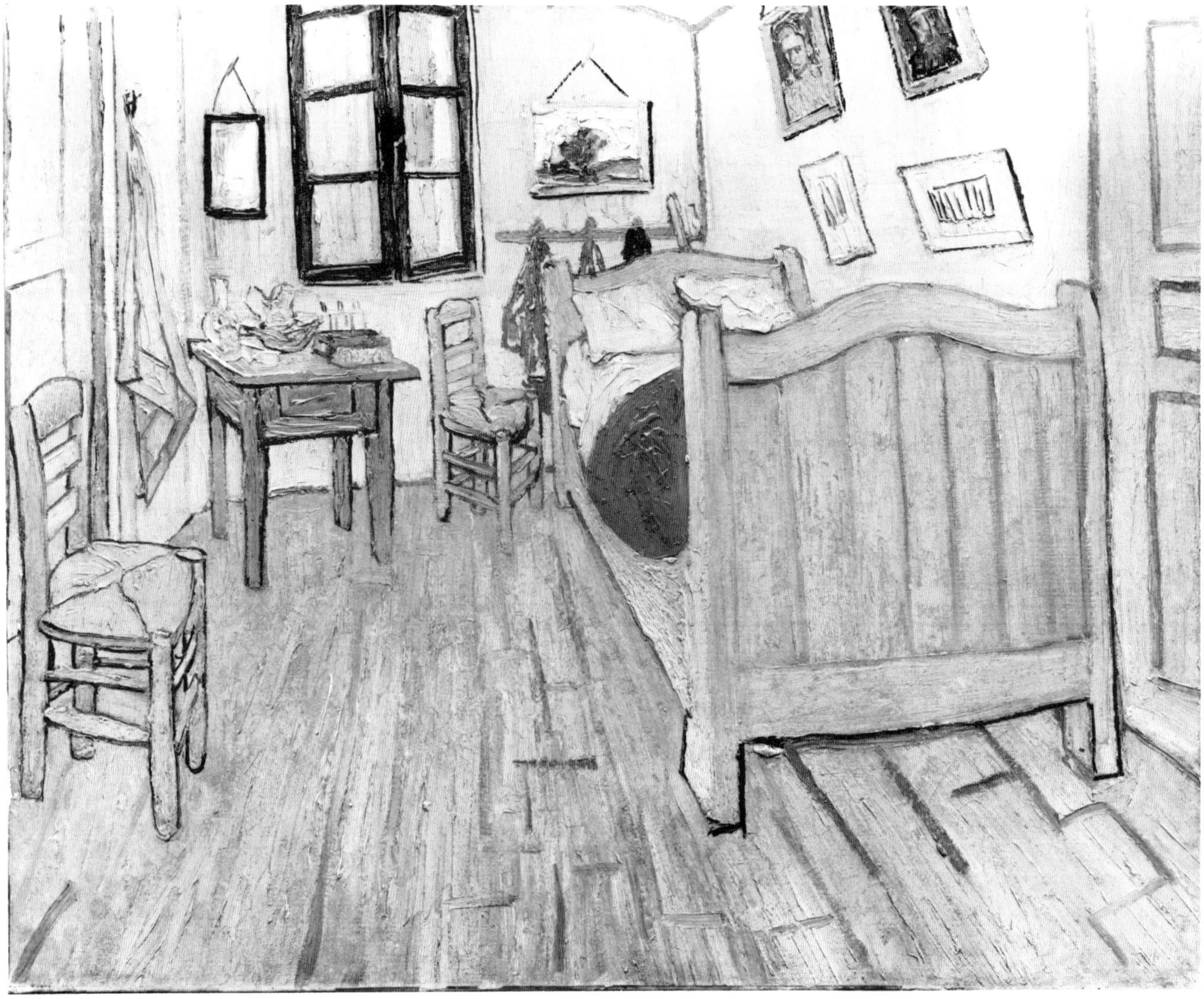

(9) *The bedroom,* Arles 1888, oil on canvas, 72 x 90 cm, Amsterdam, Rijksmuseum Vincent van Gogh.

white serving to rest the eye, this time from a vehement blue/yellow contrast, is to be found in the work '*The house at Arles*', for, in the central window of the hotel behind van Gogh's rented yellow house, there is a juxtaposition of black and white which is certainly not fortuitous. Black and white are employed in a similar manner in the painting '*The bedroom*' into which van Gogh said he wanted to introduce a "*fourth pair of complementaries*".[38]

In 1885 Gauguin spoke of "*noble tonalities*";[39] in the same year van Gogh noted Rubens' ability to "*express moods of sorrow or cheerfulness*" by means of colour, and later he found the colour of Delacroix's pictures synonymous with their meaning. Van Gogh's series of paintings on the theme of orchards were intended to communicate by means of the colours pink and green a feeling of "*astounding gaiety*".[40] From Arles van Gogh wrote that he was returning more and more to what he had been seeking even before his stay in Paris, namely "*suggestive colour*".[41]

Our understanding of the subjective dimension of colour perception is, at the present time, limited, therefore any discussion is likely to be uncertain and speculative. Despite this reservation, it is impossible, in this context, to avoid consideration of the emotional connotations of colour – van Gogh's 'suggestive colour' – altogether.

According to Herbert Read, we experience the objective qualities of colour – in technical terms their hue, saturation and luminosity – "*and then proceed to identify these qualities with our emotions*".[42] In experiments undertaken in 1908, the British psychologist Bullough demonstrated that even a single colour stimulus can provoke an aesthetic response. Bullough claims that colour possesses "*a peculiarly high suggestive power which is only rivalled by odour in diversity and precision*"; he also observes that it has a low cognitive value. A colour, therefore, "*presents at once too few and too many indications to perception and any interpretation or meaning within the limits of fancy becomes possible*".[43]

Bullough's opinions seem to be confirmed by the large number of connotations a colour such as yellow can generate: jealousy, cowardice, despair, death, mystery, grandeur, gaiety, activity, splendour or radiance. Diverse factors influence the judgement of colour: the size of the colour sample; its texture; the level of illumination; the composition of the viewing light; the state of health, age and culture of the observer. In an experiment the scientist would seek to eliminate or standardize these variables, but this is out of the question in normal encounters with works of art, consequently one would expect to find even greater variations of response in the latter situation than in the former. Many of the apparent contradictions of meaning quoted in reference to yellow would disappear if the exact shade of yellow were specified, preferably by its wavelength; for while a clear, bright, warm yellow may communicate happiness, a greener yellow may induce nausea.

Let us pause to review the variety of ways in which a painter can use colour:
naturalistically: an attempt to render the local colours of objects;
exaggeratedly: colours are based on perceived reality but are simplified and intensified;
aesthetically/syntactically: colour schemes governed by formal, harmonic and compositional factors;
expressively: colours signifying the feelings or states of mind of the artist or depicted characters;
symbolically: colours having standardised or conventional significations.
These categories are not, of course, mutually exclusive: in van Gogh's paintings one finds colours which are simultaneously based on Nature, exaggerated, aesthetic, and expressive. Whether his colours can also be regarded as symbolic depends upon how far the meanings which van Gogh intended to communicate via colour combinations are generally accepted and understood.

The copious documentation on van Gogh makes it possible to examine how a particular colour may accrete associations and acquire great significance for a painter. Colour preference tests have shown that yellow is distasteful to the majority of people; van Gogh, on the other hand, worshipped it. His predilection for yellow can be traced back to the early painting '*The Bible and French novel*' (1885). This painting depicts an open Bible which belonged to his father who had died some months before the execution of the picture. The Bible is large and

(10) *The Bible and French novel,* Nuenen 1885, oil on canvas, 65 x 78 cm, Amsterdam, Rijksmuseum Vincent van Gogh.

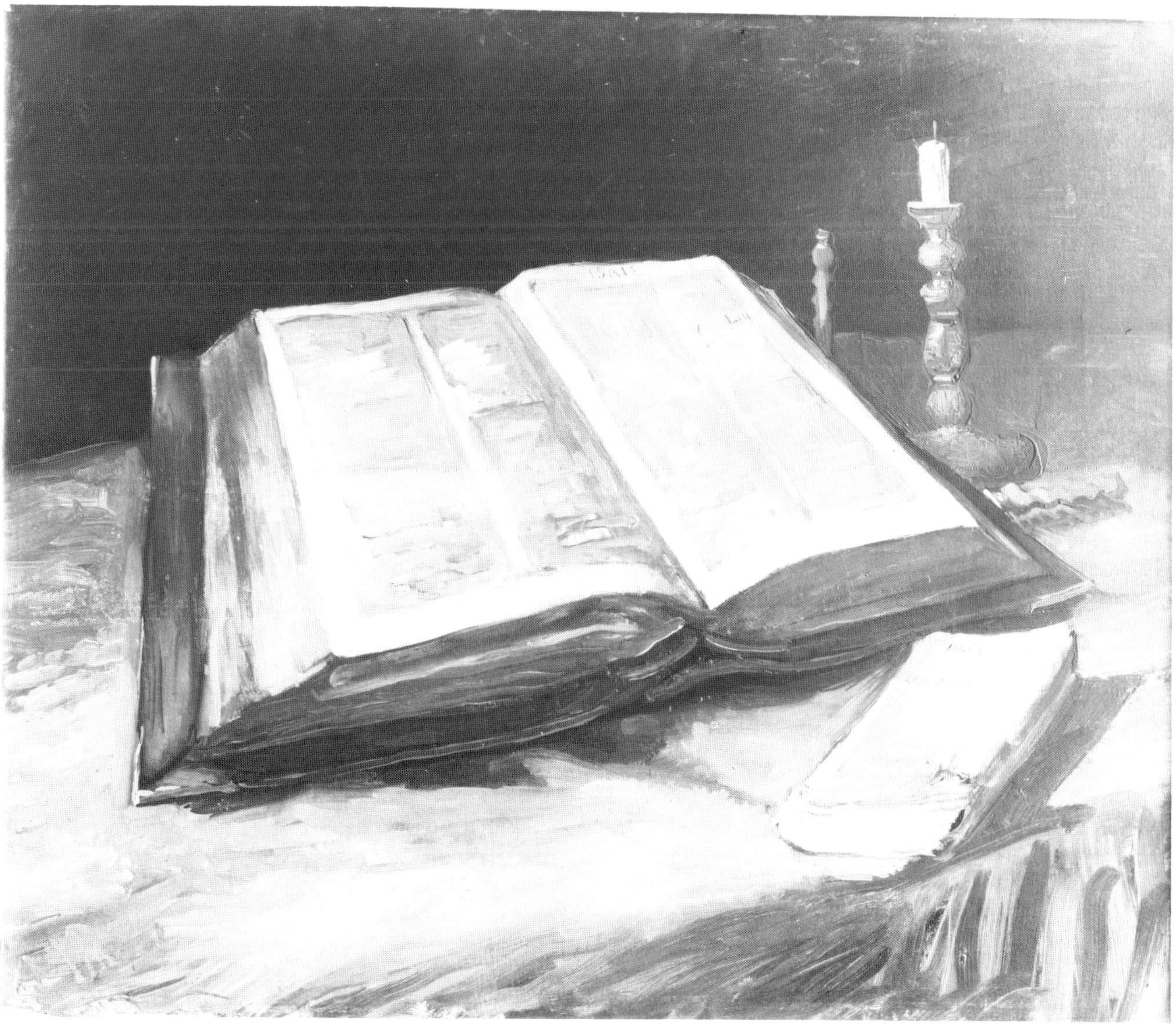

dominates the composition. Dwarfed by it, and lying near the edge of a table, is a smaller French novel. The novel, however, claims equality with the Bible by the brightness of its yellow cover. Biographical evidence enables us to identify the Bible with the pastor van Gogh and the novel with his son Vincent. French novels, in this instance Zola's *La joie de vivre*, offended the pastor hence the yellow book not only symbolizes Vincent and the energy of life but also rebellion, the struggle of son against father, the secular against the religious, the modern against the ancient.

In Japan a yellow house is symbolic of friendship. This thought was probably in van Gogh's mind when he considered founding a school of painters in the yellow house at Arles – he had some knowledge of Japanese culture and art; they had been much in vogue during his stay in Paris. His letters, written on yellow notepaper, are full of eulogies to the colour, and during the summer of 1888 he wrote that he had reached a high peak of yellow, presumably meaning that he had experienced a period of intense creativity. He compared himself to Monticelli who "*did the South all in yellow, all in orange, all in sulphur*",[44] and considered that he was continuing Monticelli's work there as if he were his son or his brother.

Yellow is the colour closest to the warmth and radiance of the sun and this meaning is the most general underlying van Gogh's fondness for it. If yellow pigment can be considered a painterly equivalent of the areas of gold leaf typical of earlier Christian altarpieces, then the colour evokes not only the sun but also the divine light of God. Van Gogh wanted to avoid overt religious imagery, consequently if a sacred meaning was to be communicated it had to be achieved by the use of brilliant colours.

The yellow of the sunflowers had, for van Gogh, a more particular meaning: "*an idea symbolizing gratitude*".[45] Van Gogh had painted sunflowers before in Paris. He used to see them in a restaurant next to his brother's place of work on the Boulevard Monmartre, thus the most probable attribution of gratitude is to Theo, the brother to whom van Gogh owed so much both financially and in terms of moral support. Again the problem arises: 'Is the meaning "gratitude" obvious to the public who view van Gogh's paintings?'. Signac for one did not see 'gratitude' in the sunflowers only "*a tomb of yellow*". To Bernard, on the other hand, they symbolized "*the brightness of love*".

At first sight, paintings such as the '*Sunflowers*' appear to be straightforward depictions of real objects, but the objects and places painted by van Gogh often have a hallucinatory quality which is due to the pressure of their hidden meanings. According to Nordenfalk, van Gogh's aim was "*to depict the things of daily life so that they conveyed the message of a higher reality*". The critic also describes several works as 'private cryptograms' which require for their elucidation a special knowledge of literary sources and a knowledge of psychology in order to reveal their underlying significance. Van Gogh may have thought of himself as an orthodox realist "*but in his eyes ... the world was not a simple matter of perception only – it was itself a 'world of images, stories, allegories'* ".[46]

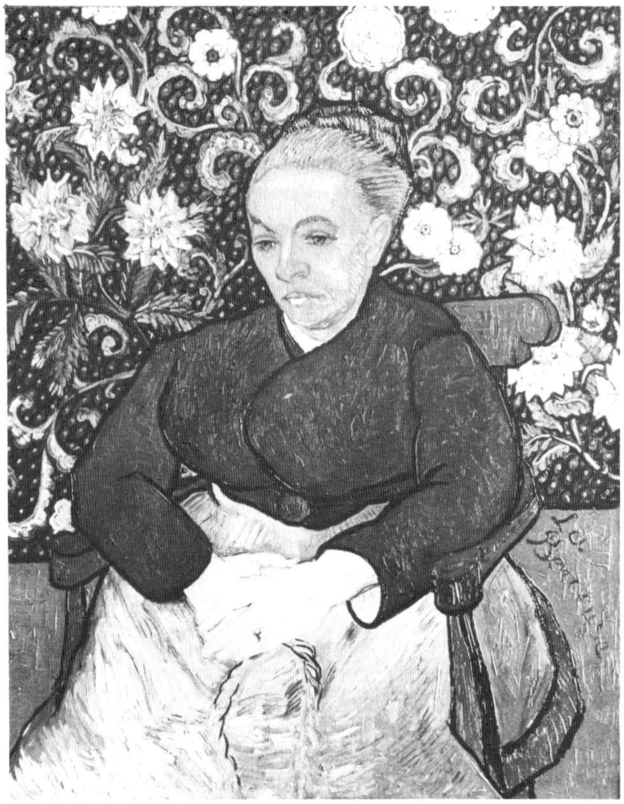

(11) *La Berceuse*, Arles 1889, oil on canvas, 92 x 73 cm, Otterlo, Rijksmuseum Kröller-Müller.

Perhaps the clearest example of an allegorical work from the Arles period is '*La Berceuse*'. This painting began as a simple portrait of Madame Roulin, the wife of van Gogh's postman friend, rocking her child to sleep (she is holding in her hand a string attached to a cradle which is not

(12) *Sketch for a decorative triptych*, St Rémy 1889, pen and ink, Letter 592 to Theo.

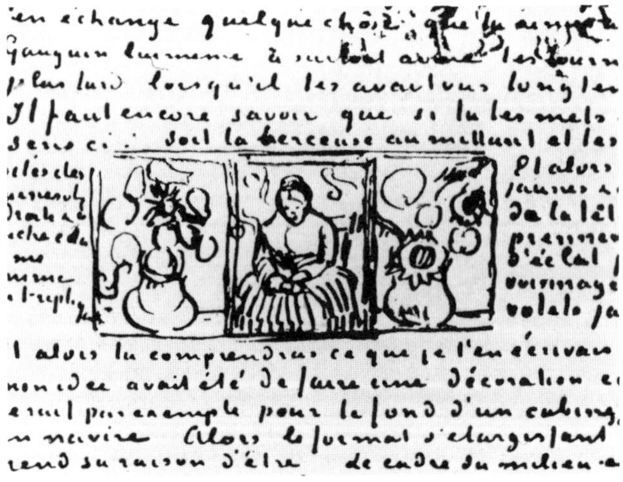

depicted in the painting). Van Gogh produced no less than five versions of this subject. By the time the fifth portrait had been completed, the idea behind the work had undergone a transformation in the mind of van Gogh: stimulated by Pierre Loti's book *Pêcheur d'Icelande* and by a Breton legend recounted by Gauguin, van Gogh imagined Madame Roulin as an apparition such as might appear to sailors while at sea. This 'vision' would serve to remind the sailors of their childhoods, of the lullabies sung by their nurses, of their mothers and wives ashore. In order to reach his sailor audience van Gogh imagined the painting displayed at the end of a ship's cabin flanked by images of sunflowers.

Van Gogh aimed to communicate his ideas without resorting to conventional symbols or literary references. Relationships of colour were to carry the meaning: "*There is an attempt to get all the* **music** *of the colour here (the South) into* ***'La Berceuse'*** *... a lullaby of colour*".[47] Remarks concerning two other symbolic pictures – '*The bedroom*' and '*The night cafe*' – repeat the same idea: "*By means of all these diverse tones I have wanted to express* **absolute restfulness**" ...[48] "*The colour is to do everything ... is to be suggestive of rest and sleep ... the squareness of the furniture will strengthen this impression of inviolable repose*".[49] Of '*The night cafe*' van Gogh wrote: "*I have tried to express the terrible passions of humanity by means of red and green*" ...[50] "*the powers of darkness ... by soft Louis XV green and malachite, contrasting with yellow-green and harsh blue-greens ... I have tried to express the idea that the cafe is a place where one can ruin oneself, go mad or commit a crime*".[51]

Portraiture was a genre in which van Gogh made much use of symbolic colour. Thus in his painting '*Reminiscence of a garden at Etten*' a figure with a colour combination of lemon-yellow and violet was symbolic of his mother's personality, while red, orange and green symbolized the personality of his sister Wilhelmina. The respective colour schemes of the two '*Chair*' paintings are also symbolic of their users: reds, greens and violets indicating Gauguin, and yellow, red and turquoise indicating van Gogh. In his portrait of a poet called Bock, van Gogh intended to communicate the sitter's profession, the very thoughts of a poet, the fact that Bock is a dreamer, and his affection for Bock, all by means of "*a light tone against a sombre background*" ...[52] "*by this simple combination of the bright head against the rich blue background, I get a mysterious effect, like a star in the depth of an azure sky*".[53]

Van Gogh's aim to replace Christian iconography by secular subjects while still retaining the glorifying function of religious art, is evident from his comments on portraiture: "*I want to paint men and women with that something of the eternal which the halo used to symbolise and which we seek to convey by the actual radiance and vibration of our colouring*".[54] Critical of the tendency towards literary symbolism in the work of the Pont-Aven School, van Gogh wrote to Bernard: "*One can try to give an impression of anguish without aiming straight at the historic garden of Gethsemane ... it is not necessary to portray the characters of the Sermon on the Mount in order to produce a consoling and gentle motif*".[55]

If one did not know van Gogh's oeuvre one might assume, from his repeated assertions of the need to express ideas by means of colour alone, that he was advocating a completely abstract kind of painting. All van Gogh's works are representational, consequently despite his remarks colour never functions in isolation from an image. This is important for the communication of van Gogh's ideas to an audience because some common language or code must exist between two people before any communication can take place. However exaggerated and schematized van Gogh's images are, they are recognisible to anyone familiar with the perspectival representations of reality typical of Western European culture. A bedroom is a place of rest and sleep, consequently the idea of 'repose' is conveyed by a drawing of a bedroom. Some kinds of colour combination are generally perceived as calm, harmonious, and others as being energetic, disharmonious. It is obvious that if the former were used in a drawing of a bedroom, the idea of rest would be reinforced, and if the latter were used the idea of rest would be contradicted.

Van Gogh's paintings and drawings have become extremely popular in the twentieth century. This suggests that van Gogh has managed to commun-

(13) *Portrait of Eugene Bock,* Arles 1888, oil on canvas, 60 x 45 cm, Paris, The Louvre.

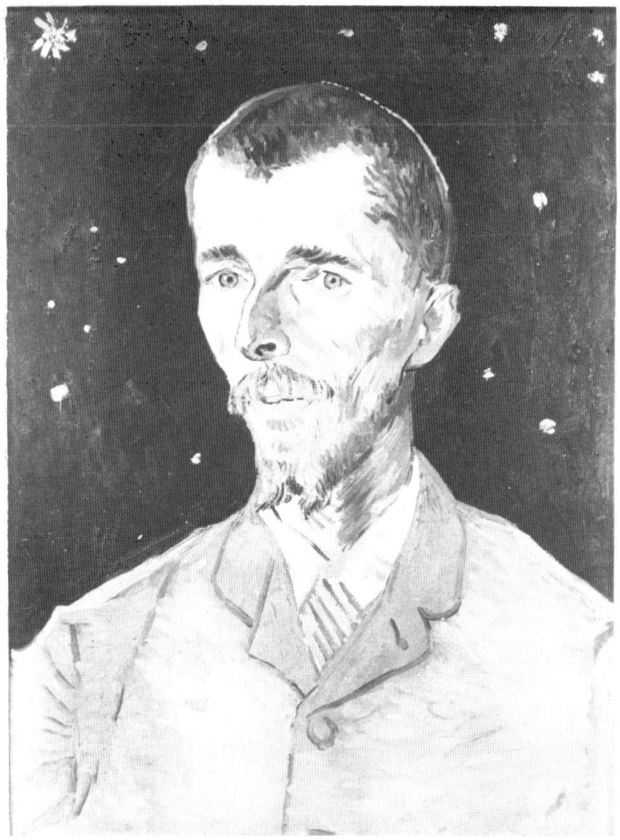

icate his ideas to a wide cross-section of the public. If his colour meanings were simply a private code it seems unlikely that van Gogh's work could have achieved such popularity (though, of course, it is possible for people to learn the codes devised by others). One explanation of van Gogh's ability to communicate with ordinary people is the fact that he often employed already popular images or cultural signs (such as an empty chair or pair of shoes signifying the absent or dead owner). Van Gogh obtained his images from three sources: (1) direct observation of contemporary reality; (2) popular illustrated magazines; and (3), paintings and reproductions of works by artists whom he admired. What van Gogh distrusted were images that were the result of pure imagination and also images based upon traditional Christian and Mythological iconography.

In regard to colour, I propose that van Gogh utilized representational imagery of a popular kind to establish the specific meaning to be communicated, and also patterns of colour combinations which are 'popular' because they are rooted in the physical/physiological basis of our perception of colour. Any remaining ambiguities and refinements of meaning are then resolved by reference to the letters, knowledge of which is now almost as widespread as knowledge of the paintings themselves.

I will end with another quotation. Writing to Theo from Antwerp in the Winter of 1885/86 van Gogh observed: "*What colour is in a picture, enthusiasm is in life*".[56]

Notes and references:

(1) Van Gogh painted five oil studies under the guidance of Anton Mauve in December 1881 but he did not begin to paint in earnest until the summer of 1882.
(2) Letter 221. All letters cited are from *The complete letters of Vincent van Gogh* (Thames and Hudson, 1958).
(3) Letter 371.
(4) Letter 233.
(5) Simultaneous contrast: when a colour stimulus is placed alongside a grey, the grey tends to take on the complementary colour of the stimulus. Another term commonly used is 'induction'. It is evident that the strongest colour contrast will occur between two complementary colours, for example, red and green, because they will mutually enhance one another.
(6) These books were: *Les artistes de mon temps* and *Grammaire des arts et dessin* by C. Blanc; *Les maîtres d'autre fois* by E. Fromentin; *Souvenirs de Gigoux* by J. F. Gigoux; *Du dessin et de la couleur* by F. Braquemond; an article on Delacroix by Th. Silvestre; an article on the Salon of 1885 in *Les temps* by P. Manz; and *L'art au XVIII siècle* by E. and J. de Goncourt.
(7) Letter 370.
(8) Letter 429.
(9) Ibid.
(10) Letter 428.
(11) C. Derkert 'Theory and practice in van Gogh's Dutch painting' *Swedish van Gogh studies* (Stockholm, 1948).
(12) Letter 371.
(13) J. Laver *Whistler* (London, 1930; 2nd ed 1951)
(14) Letter 442.
(15) A. S. Hartrick *A painter's pilgrimage through fifty years* (Cambridge, 1939).
(16) Letter 626.
(17) Letter 21 (to Bernard).
(18) Letter 459.
(19) Letter 477a (to Russell).
(20) Ibid.
(21) Letter 22 (to Wilhelmina).
(22) Letter 524.
(23) Letter 520.
(24) A. Ehrenzweig *The psychoanalysis of artistic vision and hearing* (1953) (NY: G. Braziller, 2nd ed. 1965).
(25) Letter 476.
(26) Letter 527. Van Gogh derived the term 'halo' from Chevreul whose description of the 'aureole' was cited by Blanc in *Grammaire des arts et dessin.*
(27) C. J. R. Frankl 'How Cézanne saw and used colour' *The listener* October 1951.
(28) Letter 589.
(29) Letter 497.
(30) Letter 6 (to Bernard).
(31) R. Arnheim *Art and visual perception* (Faber & Faber, 1956).
(32) Letter 526.
(33) Letter 15 (to Bernard).
(34) E. Jacobson *Basic colour* (Chicago: Theobald, 1948).
(35) *The life and work of Vincent van Gogh* (Elek, 1953).
(36) Letter 6 (to Bernard).
(37) Letter 7 (to Bernard).
(38) Letter 22 (to Gauguin).
(39) Letter to Schuffenecker quoted in *Post-Impressionism from van Gogh to Gauguin* by John Rewald.
(40) Letter 473.
(41) Letter 539.
(42) H. Read *Education through art* (Faber & Faber, 3rd rev. ed., 1956).
(43) 'The "perceptive problem" in the aesthetic appreciation of single colours' *British Journal of Psychology* 1908.
(44) Letter 8 (to Wilhelmina).
(45) Letter 20 (to Wilhelmina), and letter 626a (to Aurier).
(46) C. Nordenfalk 'Van Gogh and literature' *Journal of the Warburg and Courtauld institutes* vol 10, 1947.
(47) Letter 571(a) (to Koning).
(48) Letter 22 (to Gauguin).
(49) Letter 554.
(50) Letter 533.
(51) Letter 534.
(52) Letter 531.
(53) Letter 520.
(54) Letter 531.
(55) Letter 21 (to Bernard).
(56) Letter 443.

IN SEARCH OF
VAN GOGH'S MOTIFS IN PROVENCE

In February 1888 Vincent van Gogh arrived from Paris at the main railway station of Arles-sur-Rhône. The town of Arles, once the Roman capital of Provence, is situated twenty miles from the Mediterranean in the centre of a flat, marshy plain. Close to the Rhône the plain is fertile but elsewhere, there are tracts of arid soil. The area suffers extremes of temperature and torrential rainstorms only temporarily alleviate the discomforts caused by clouds of insects and mosquitoes; but the most severe climatic feature is the vicious wind which blows down the river valley from the north, the infamous Mistral. Though Arles has grown over the centuries, and now houses a population of over 40,000, the sky-line is still dominated by the Roman amphitheatre, scene of the annual bull-fight, one of the few remaining links with a past rich in ritual (Christian and pagan), rich in costume and legend, a past proudly and diligently commemorated in the local Arlaten museum. This was the town chosen by Van Gogh as the centre for a School of painting in the South.

In choosing Arles, Vincent wished to emulate his idols Delacroix and Monticelli.[1] The former had gone all the way to Africa in search of colour and the latter had worked in Marseilles. Vincent was also intrigued by the reputation of the Arlésiennes who were famous for their beauty and traditional costume, and indeed by the whole of the picturesque Provençal life, described by Daudet in his novels. Provence was in many ways a promised land, a kind of ideal Holland with over-tones of Japan; being flat, pastoral and, most important, warmer than the North. Ironically, when Vincent arrived Provence was covered by snow; undeterred by the elements, Vincent produced his first landscape (or snowscape) showing Arles in the distance. This ancient and melancholy town was the scene of Vincent's greatest masterpieces and also his most excruciating personal humiliations.

On his arrival, Vincent walked into the town and found a room at 30, Rue Cavalerie, the Hotel-Restaurant Carrel. It is probable that an early canvas depicting meal-time in a restaurant is of the dining room at the Hotel Carrel; in it one can see the simple, rush-seated chairs common to the district, and similar to those he was to buy to furnish his own house. One of these chairs later formed the subject of a symbolic self-portrait; a companion piece to a painting of a rather more elaborate chair used by Gauguin. Examples of both types of chair are preserved in the Arlaten museum.

Rue Cavalerie still exists but the Hotel Carrel has been replaced by modern buildings, as has the butchers shop across the street which Vincent painted shortly after his arrival. A little way along the same street is the church of Saint Julien, the spire of which he drew across the rooftops from his attic window, a drawing reminiscent of other attic views made in Holland and Paris.

Finding it difficult to paint in the Hotel, Vincent rented a small yellow-coloured house, number 2, Place Lamartine, which faced south across the large square between the railway station and the city gate. Unfortunately the house was destroyed in the last war and now the only obvious reminder of Vincent's residence are two hotels named after him and his companion Gauguin. At night, in Place Lamartine, one can hear the sounds of the trains shunting, just as Vincent must have heard them before falling asleep. Perhaps these sounds encouraged him to paint the little-reproduced study of wagons in the marshalling yards nearby.

Vincent's drawings of the square in 1888 show that it possessed a small central garden and pond. These have now given way to the needs of the automobile and it is necessary to stand in the middle of the road in order to study the motif of the famous '*Yellow House*' painting from the spot where Vincent set up his easel. Although nothing of the yellow house remains, the large building that overshadows it in the painting is still standing and on its right are the two railway bridges which Vincent painted subsequently as a subject in themselves. The yellow house was used as a studio for several months while Vincent awaited funds from Theo to furnish it thoroughly. Meantime Vincent slept at the Café de l'Alcazar situated at the eastern end of Place Lamartine; it too has been demolished. This café remained open all night and Vincent stayed up for three nights to record the interior with its blood red walls and green billiard table ('*Night Café*').

A few steps from the site of the yellow house are the banks of the Rhône. A curve in the river enables one to see, silhouetted above the torpid water, the belfreys and spires of Arles. Here Vincent painted many river scenes, for example, '*Boats unloading sand*', '*View of the Trinquetaille bridge*' and '*Starry night*'. The legend has it that Vincent wore lighted candles in his hat in order to paint this latter canvas. In his painting '*Collier boats moored to the quay*', Vincent depicted the church of Saint Pierre on the west bank of the Rhône against a highly coloured sunset. He frequently painted the Trinquetaille bridge, linking Arles with the west bank, in the background of his river scenes. One study of steps leading from the river embankment to the bridge, shows in the foreground a delicate sapling; it is now fully grown. The original ironwork of the bridge itself has been replaced because of war damage.

Vincent was not friendless in Arles, his most intimate relationship was with the Roulin family, all of whom provided subjects for portraits. Roulin worked as a postman unloading mail at the railway station just around the corner from Vincent's house.

When Paul Gauguin joined Vincent in Arles visits were arranged to places of public entertainments: to the bull-fight in the Roman amphitheatre, to the brothel for the sake of "*hygiene*"; two rather sketchy canvases remain of these expeditions. They also visited the famous avenue of Roman tombs known as '*Les Alyscamps*', to observe the promenading Arlésiennes and to paint several studies of motifs unchanged for many centuries.

On either side of the town's main east-to-west boulevard, now crowded with the cars of the tourists, are two quiet public parks, the '*Garden of summer*' and the '*Garden of winter*', where pensioners relax in the sun on wooden benches. This typically Impressionist scene formed the subject of a whole series of delightful pictures. Just off the main boulevard is a small square, Place du Forum, where Vincent painted the well-known '*Café Terrace*'.

The café is now a shop but the site is still clearly recognizable. Close to the Place du Forum is the Hotel-Dieu where Vincent was admitted after his first mental breakdown and again when a petition by the local citizens demanded his removal because they considered him a public danger. The courtyard and small formal garden of the hospital is still much as Vincent painted it.

The environs of Arles are criss-crossed by numerous canals and skirting the southern limit of the town is a major canal where Vincent painted several of his most beautiful canvases. In 1888 the canal was spanned by attractive drawbridges with white wooden superstructures identical in construction to those which can be seen in Amsterdam. Besides their obvious appeal to a painter's eye and the nostalgic memories they evoked in Vincent, they provided a comparison with Japan, for in Paris Vincent had copied Japanese prints depicting peasants crossing wooden bridges. Today only one bridge, the familiar Pont de l'Anglois, remains in working order and is still frequented by the fishermen and pairs of strolling lovers mentioned in Vincent's letters. Here, on the edge of the country, one can share the silence and solitude Vincent expressed in the limpid beauty of his bridge series.

From the tall reeds that grow in the ditches and canals of Provence, Vincent made reed pens of different widths in imitation of Japanese artists. The range of textural effects that a major artist can achieve with these pens is quite remarkable. The dots, hatches and patterns of Vincent's drawings seem to reflect a kind of colour code similar to that used in heraldry, though in his case an intuitive one.

From Place Lamartine Vincent used to set out, early in the morning, loaded with painting materials in search of motifs appropriate to the season, orchards in spring, harvests in summer ... His motifs are therefore, of necessity, within walking distance of the yellow house, and even now the open countryside is only half-a-mile from Place Lamartine. While it is not always possible to identify particular motifs, the gardens, fields and vineyards abound with his subjects – cherry trees, pear trees, apricot trees, irises, sunflowers and cypresses.

Through the two railway bridges in Place Lamartine runs the road to Tarascon, still shaded by plane trees, where Vincent painted a portrait of himself on a typical painting expedition. He often took this road to visit his painter acquaintances Mourier-Peterson (a Dane) and MacNight (an American) at the village of Fontvielle. Alphonse Daudet is associated with this village and Vincent could not resist drawing the Moulin de Daudet.

If, instead of following the Tarascon road, one walks parallel to the railway embankment, one soon discovers a low communicating tunnel (to be seen in the background of one canvas of plane trees). Through the tunnel is a rather unimpressive muddy stream which flows past the town's gasworks. The stream, called '*La Roubine de Roi*', was used by the women of Arles for washing clothes. There is a canvas by Vincent of the Arlésiennes at their chores with the chimney and buildings of the gasworks in the middle distance. The path here is merely a rough track which follows the stream past luxuriant orchards and vineyards, until suddenly there are open fields as far as the eye can see. Against the sky in the north are the low blue hills of the Alpilles, but these are insignificant in comparison to the vast extent of the plain known as '*La Crau*'.

This is a most extraordinary place, for in all directions are Vincent's subjects. The Vigueirat canal spanned by a low bridge with two stone arches, is the motif of one of the first Arles landscapes. Beyond the stream, in the distance, are the ruins of a Benedictine abbey called Mont Majour and a small but distinctive rocky hill called '*Mont de Cordes*'. These two details enable one to identify the scene of Vincent's '*Harvest*' painting. The sensation of having stepped into one of his pictures is perhaps never so intense as here among the fields of waving corn. With the motif in front of one and a reproduction of the Harvest painting to hand, one can observe clearly how Vincent departed from the kind of reality recorded by the camera. The 'distortions' are typical of most of the Arles studies: the landscape is "tipped up" towards the picture plane, perspective lines are greatly exaggerated and objects in the middle and far distances are enlarged beyond their optical image size to compensate for the psychological effect known as size constancy. When one tries to photograph his motifs it becomes even more obvious that his paintings were not constructed from a single fixed viewpoint but combine several in the one canvas, thus there is never a one-to-one correspondence between photograph and painting.

Looking back the way we have come, the ancient, serrated profile of Arles appears to float above the white and pink orchards like a fabled city. In fact in 1888 Arles must have been a rather squalid provincial town (Gauguin thought it a paltry place and filthy), but from this viewpoint it is easy to sympathise with Vincent's image of Arles as an idyllic "*miniature Rome*". Arles appears in this familiar guise in the background of many of the Provençal landscapes and in some it is possible, from the characteristic church towers and such details as railway lines and windmills, to pinpoint, with a fair degree of accuracy, the spot where Vincent set up his easel.

Vincent and his friend the Zouave officer Milliet often went on foot to the rocky hillside of Mont Majour to sketch. Milliet was willing to respect Vincent's advice concerning the art of drawing but did not appreciate his method of direct oil painting. Several drawings remain of the ruined abbey, of trees clinging precariously to the rock face and of the Mont de Cordes a short distance away to the east, looking like an upturned boat among the fields of La Crau. These intensely cultivated fields seem to have fascinated Vincent, judging from the obsessive detail with which he drew them, and it is probable that he painted the monumental '*Sower*' pictures in this locality.

Amy Oakley describes a similar walk from Arles to Mont Majour and how she scrambled over rocks and undergrowth to reach the Mont de Cordes said to have been occupied and fortified by the Saracens in the eighth century.[2] The Mont de Cordes appears on the horizon of many of Vincent's landscapes and must have reminded him of the coal slag heaps of the Borinage where he first discovered his vocation as an artist.

In Provence at this time short local journeys were made by stagecoach. Vincent, loath to leave such an attractive motif untouched, made a study of the Tarascon diligence in red and green. In June 1888 Vincent travelled south by coach to Les Saintes-Maries-de-la-mer, a small fishing port on the Mediterranean. Still the largest building in this picturesque town, is the curious church which Vincent painted and drew from a viewpoint on the low sea wall; another motif which is still perfectly intact.

He also made drawings and oil studies of the small thatched huts typical of the Camargue and used by the horsemen known as 'the Guardians'. Other canvases depict fishing boats on the shore, or moving swiftly on the glittering water. Vincent obviously enjoyed the challenge of rendering the turbulence of the sea, and the colour of the shallow water is seen to be the very green he painted it, whereas previously one might have thought this colour an example of artistic licence. These beach scenes are reminiscent of those Vincent made at Scheveningen in Holland where he first drew the seashore.

On May 3rd 1889 Vincent voluntarily committed himself to the asylum of St. Paul, just outside the village of Saint-Rémy which is situated fifteen miles north-east of Arles among the hills which appear so often on the horizon of the Arles landscapes.

The asylum building and large park with its tall pine trees and borders of irises, were immediately recorded by Vincent with his usual need to familiarise himself completely with his surroundings. The park is now neglected and overgrown. In the long grass are the ever-present cicadas, their shrill noise reminds one of Vincent's small drawings of them.

He was allotted a cell on the upper floor of the asylum and naturally had to spend a good deal of his time confined to this cheerless room, especially in bad weather. The window of his cell formed a natural perspective frame and looked out on to a sloping wheatfield (now a vegetable garden) beyond which are olive groves and mountains. He painted this view many times during rain and under full sunlight: the well-known '*Reaper*' pictures are of this field. The only thing Vincent omitted from these paintings were the bars of his cell.

When Vincent was well enough he was permitted excursions outside the asylum and in November 1889 he visited Saint-Rémy to paint two canvases of road-menders at work on the main boulevard. The hospital buildings overlooked Saint-Rémy and from this vantage point Vincent made his drawings for the extraordinary painting '*Starry Night*', which shows the village beneath a vast, swirling heaven. In this region cypresses are especially common. When one sees those tall, green-black trees twisting like flames in the Mistral one realises that the contorted shapes of Vincent's cypresses are not unduly exaggerated. Several motifs in the nearby mountains, such as '*Entrance to a quarry*', can be identified but generally it is difficult to pinpoint many of the Saint-Rémy motifs outside the asylum walls because of the lack of characteristic architectural details. Nevertheless, the whole landscape of olive groves, distorted rocks, narrow ravines and caverns appears to echo Vincent's vision.

Today the asylum of St. Paul is closed and its windows covered by wooden shutters. The pervading air of solitariness seems to symbolise the past human tragedy of the patients. Once Vincent heard "*terrible cries and howls as of beasts in a menagerie*" and now, during storms, the asylum is lit by flashes of lightning, and is filled by the sound of thunder and the dry rattle of the shutters, then Vincent's 'madness' seems no more extreme than Nature's.

Art historians such as Tralbaut and Rewald have photographed most of the existing motifs but admirers of Van Gogh's oeuvre should try to visit Provence for themselves.[3] Many things will disappoint, such as the lack of interest in the painter in Arles itself, the only official memorial to him being a small room in the Arlatan museum decorated with poor reproductions and a street named '*Avenue Van Gogh*'. His house, bombed in 1944, looks from photographs of the ruin as if it could have been restored if anyone had shown initiative. It is left to the commercial interests, hotels bearing his name and shops selling coloured postcards,to pay a tainted homage.

The importance of visual reality to Van Gogh's creative process cannot be over-emphasised, Gauguin had encouraged him to work from memory but Vincent found this kind of 'abstraction' unsatisfactory. It is not possible to recapture before the motifs the kind of emotion they stimulated in Vincent, indeed many of the scenes are trite and insignificant, or too obviously picturesque for modern taste. The lesson of the motifs is to emphasize once again the extraordinary nature of Van Gogh's personality which brought to relatively banal scenes an originality of vision rarely equalled in the history of painting.

Notes and references:

(1) For a discussion of the influence of Monticelli see A. Sheon 'Monticelli and van Gogh' *Apollo* 85 (64) June 1967 pp 444–8.

(2) A. Oakley *The heart of Provence* (NY: Appleton, 1936).

(3) Books and articles containing photographs of motifs and dealing with the Provençal period are as follows:

W. J. de Gruyter *The world of van Gogh* (photography by E. Andriesse) (NY: Holbein, 1953).

P. J. Pollack 'What Vincent saw' *Chicago art bulletin* 44 (1) February 1950 pp 5–9.

J. Rewald 'The artist and the land' *Art News annual* 19 1950 pp 64–73.

J. Rewald 'Van Gogh en Provence' *L'Amour de l'art* 17 1936 pp 289–298.

M. E. Tralbaut *Van Gogh: a pictorial biography* (Thames & Hudson, 1959).

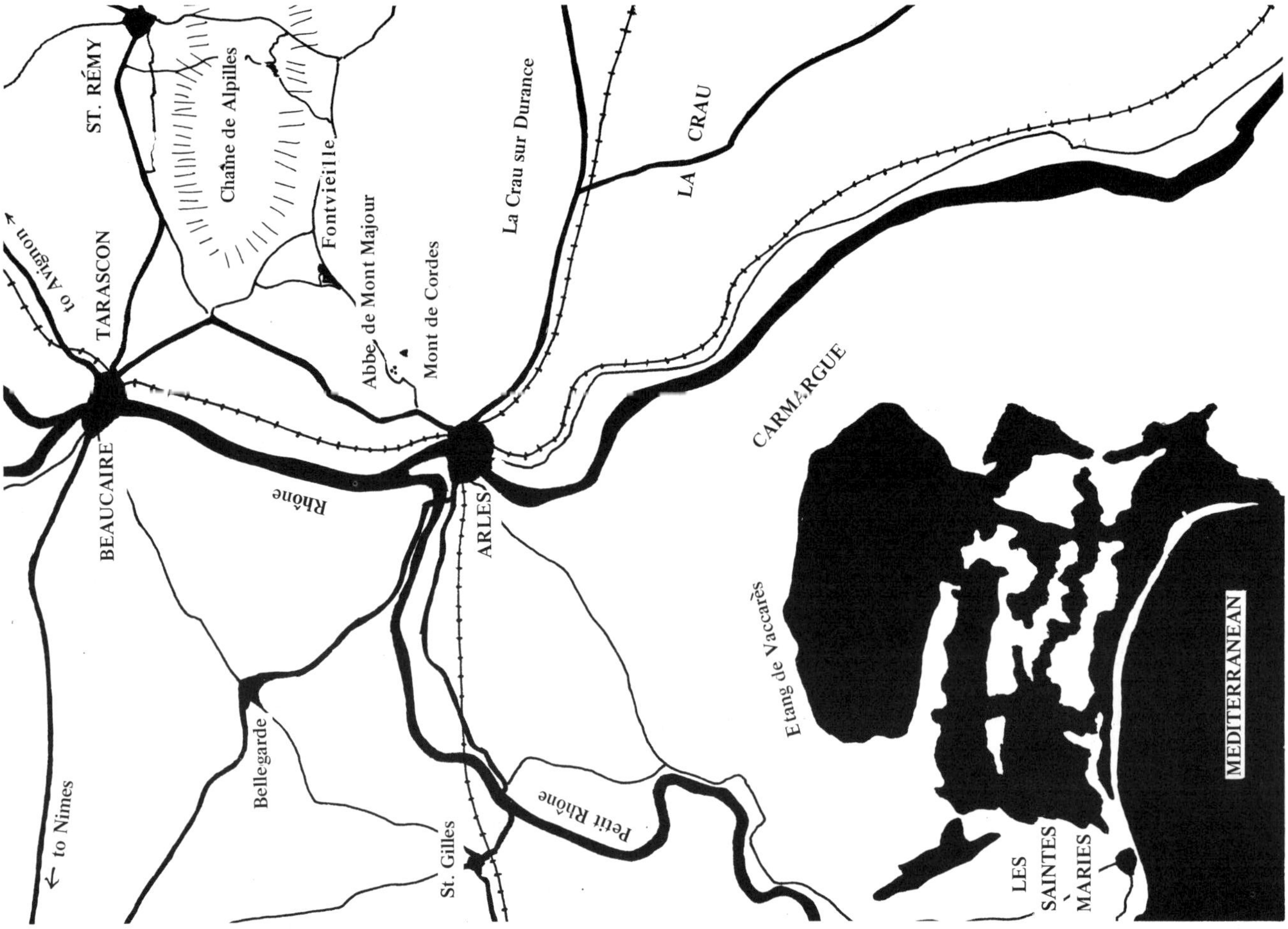

(14) *Map of Provence showing the region around Arles.*

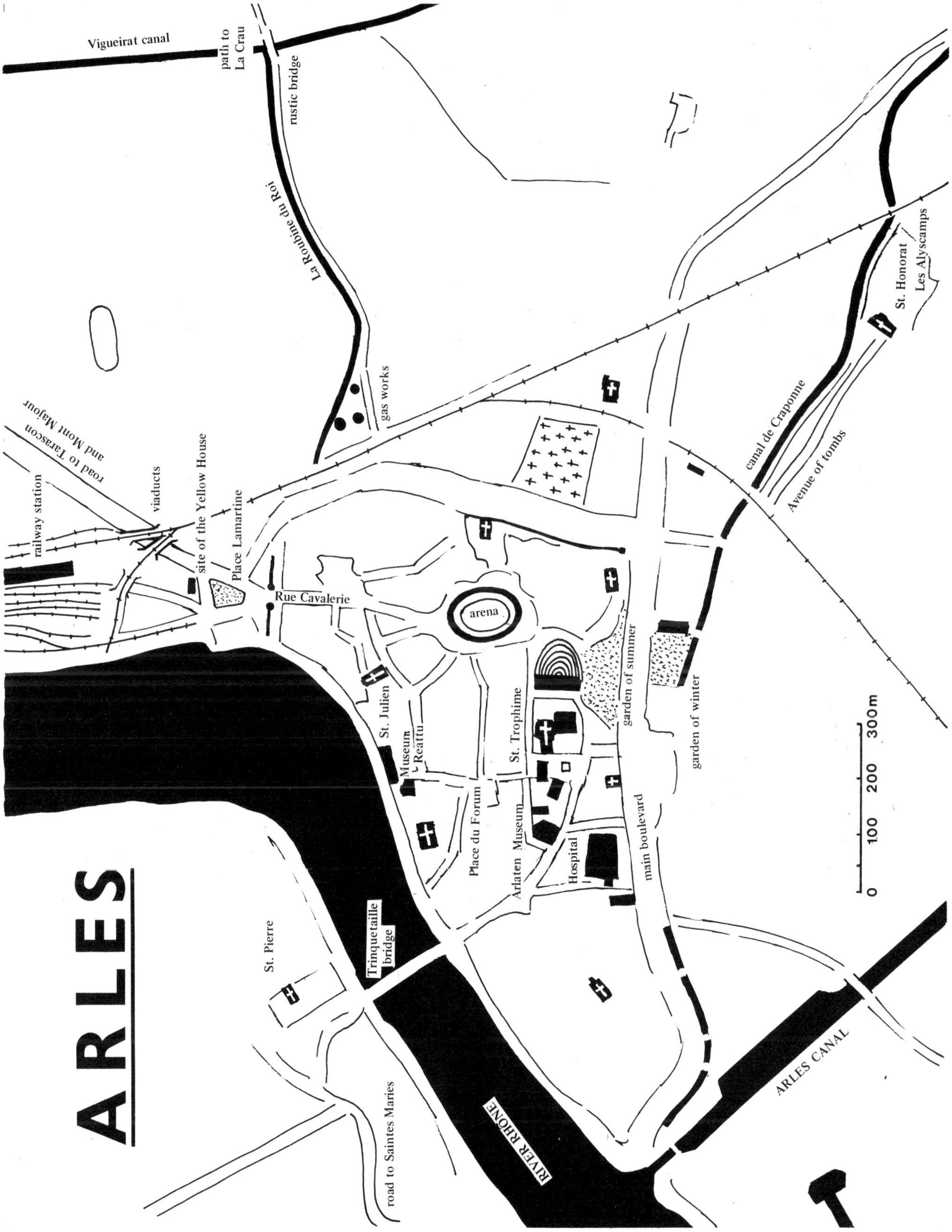

(**15**) *Map of Arles.*

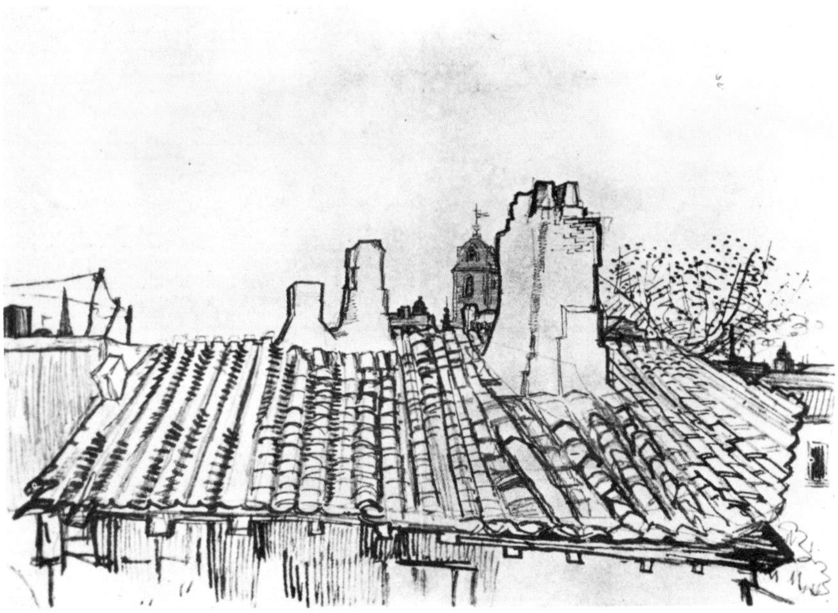

(16) *Tiled roof with chimneys and St Julien's church tower,* **Arles 1888, pencil, pen and ink, 25.5 x 34.5 cm, Paris, Galerie Berggruen.**

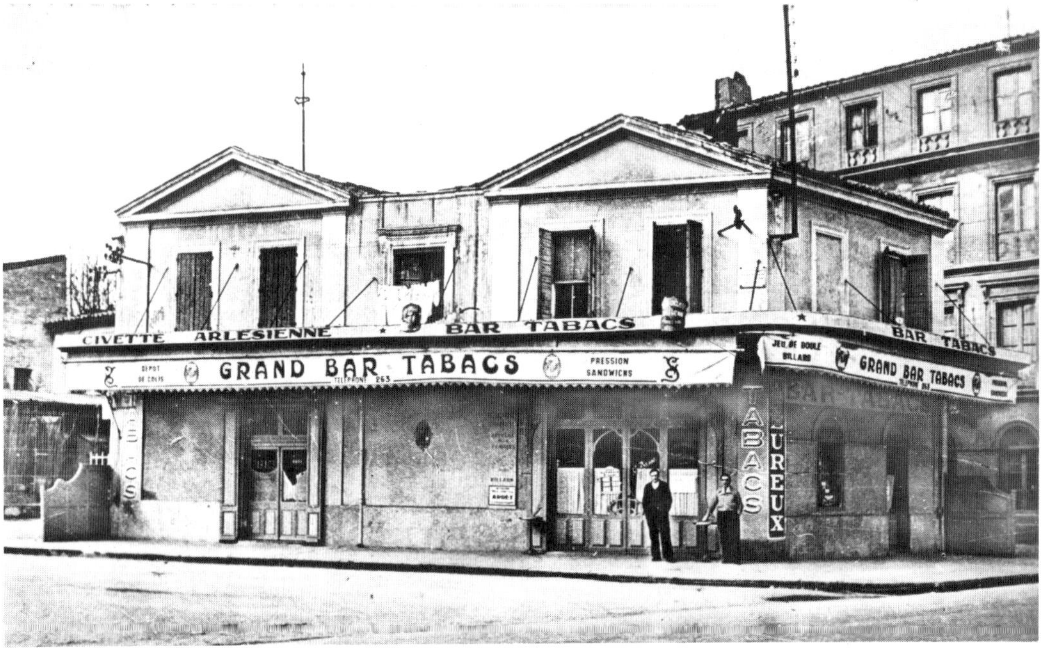

(17) *Photograph of the yellow house*

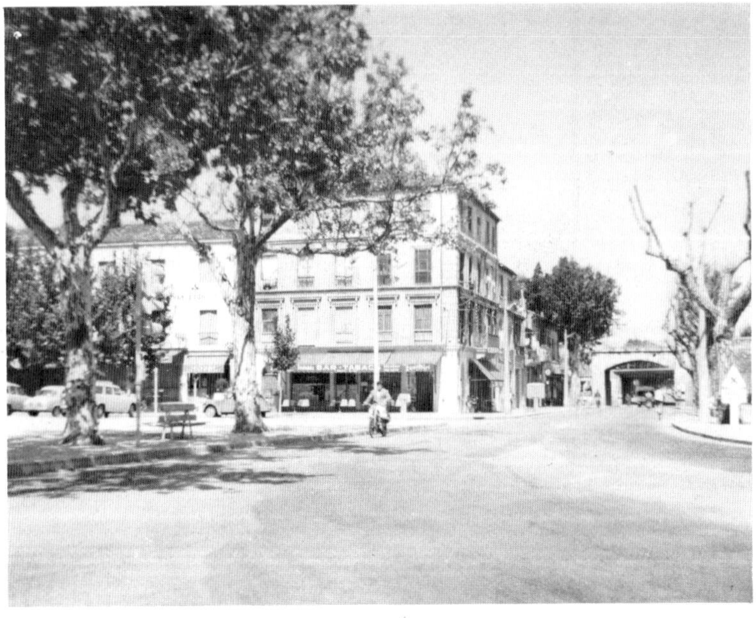

(18) *Site of the yellow house.*

(19) *Unloading boats,* **Arles 1888, oil on canvas, 71 x 95 cm, Location unknown.**

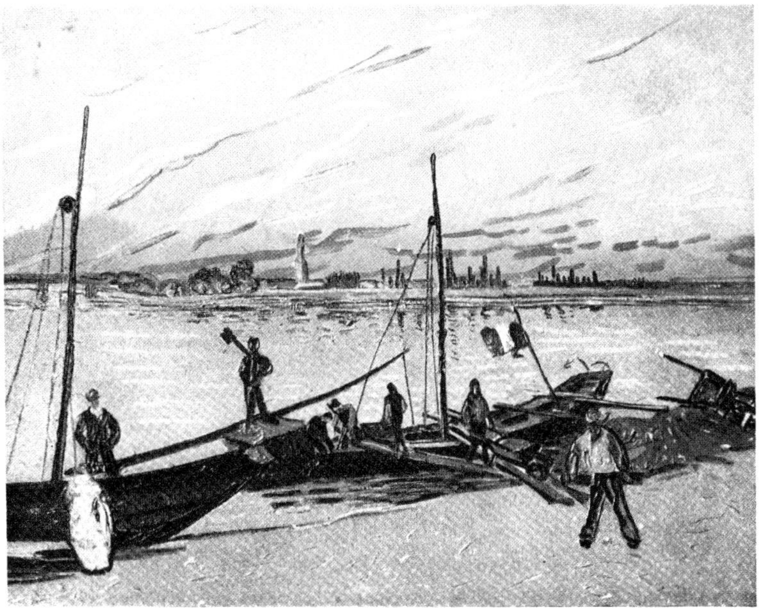

(20)
Railway carriages,
**Arles 1888,
oil on canvas,
45 x 50 cm,
Location unknown.**

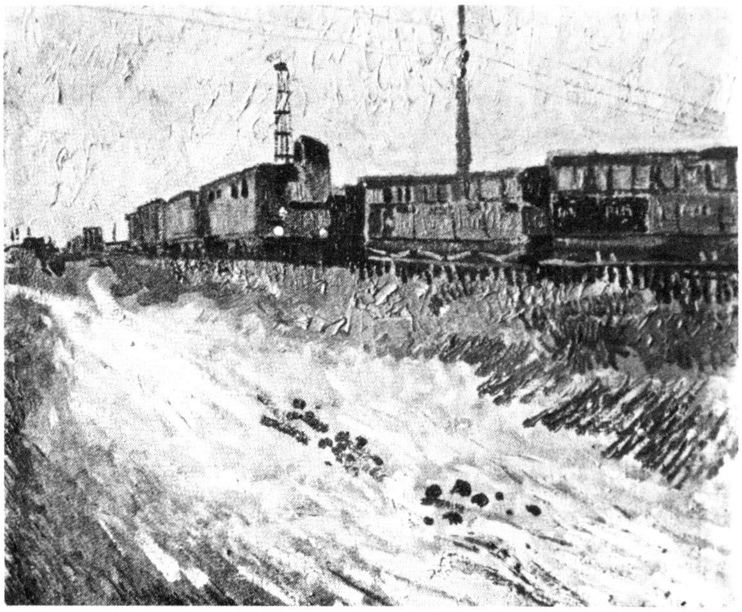

(21) *Railway wagons.*

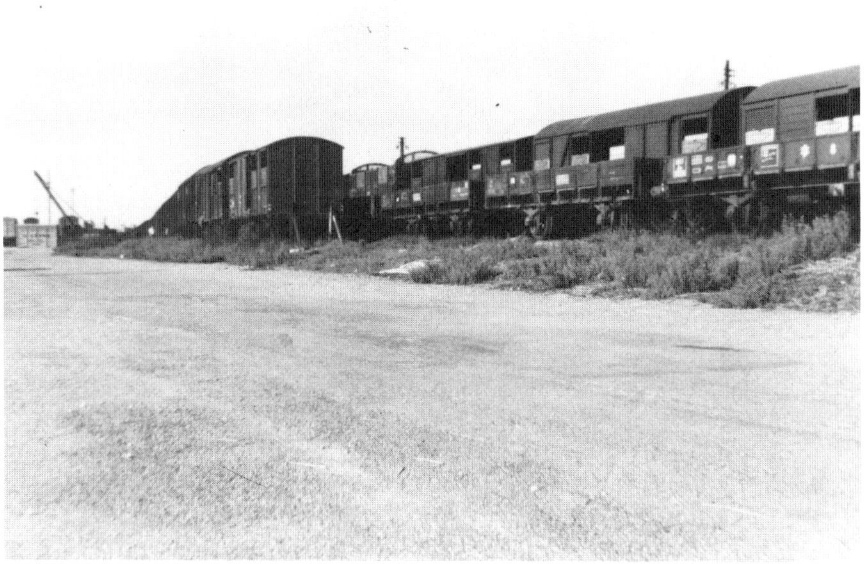

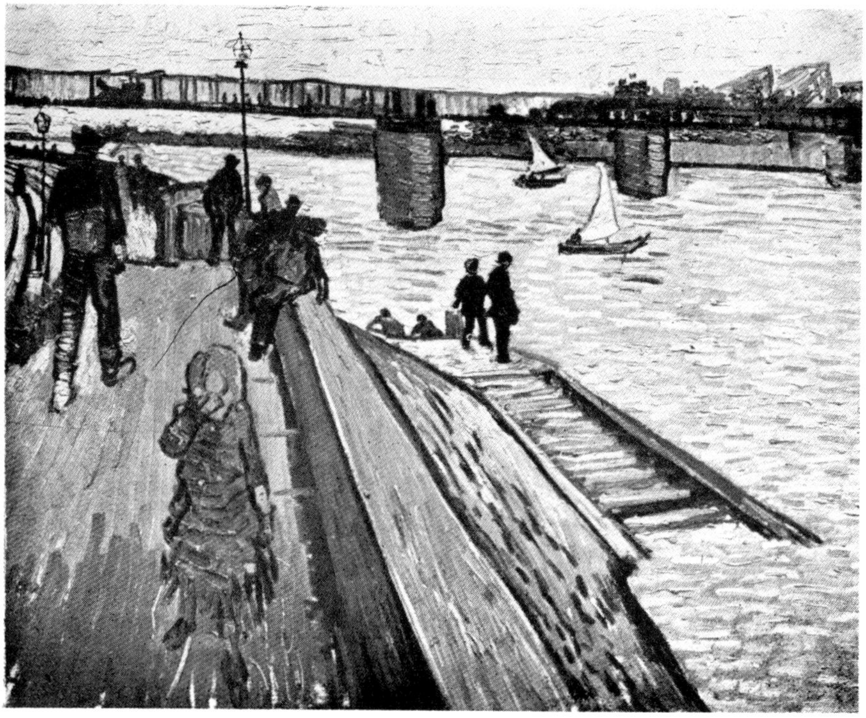

(22) *View of the river Rhône with Trinquetaille bridge,* **Arles 1888, oil on canvas, 65 x 81 cm, Location unknown.**

(23) *The river Rhône and Trinquetaille bridge.*

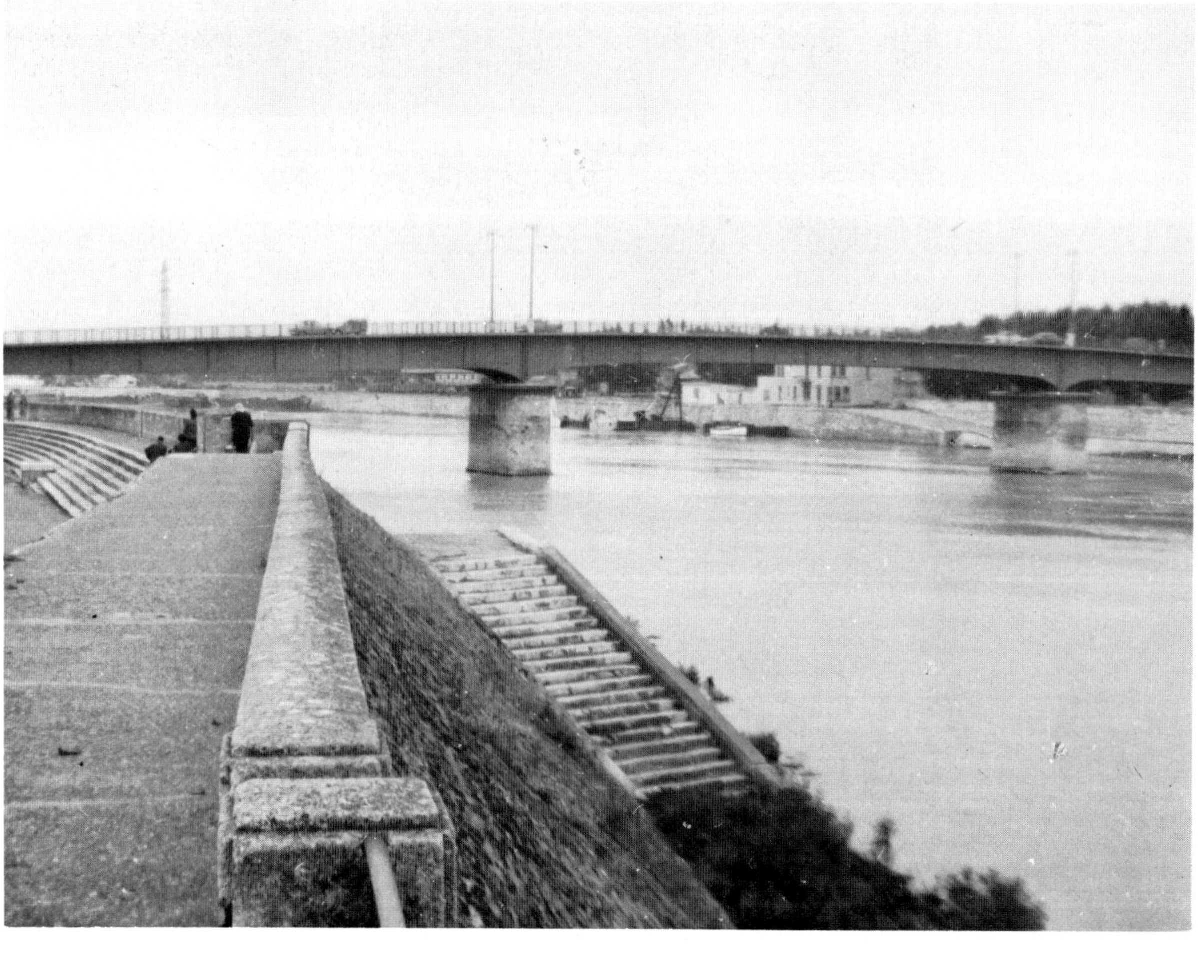

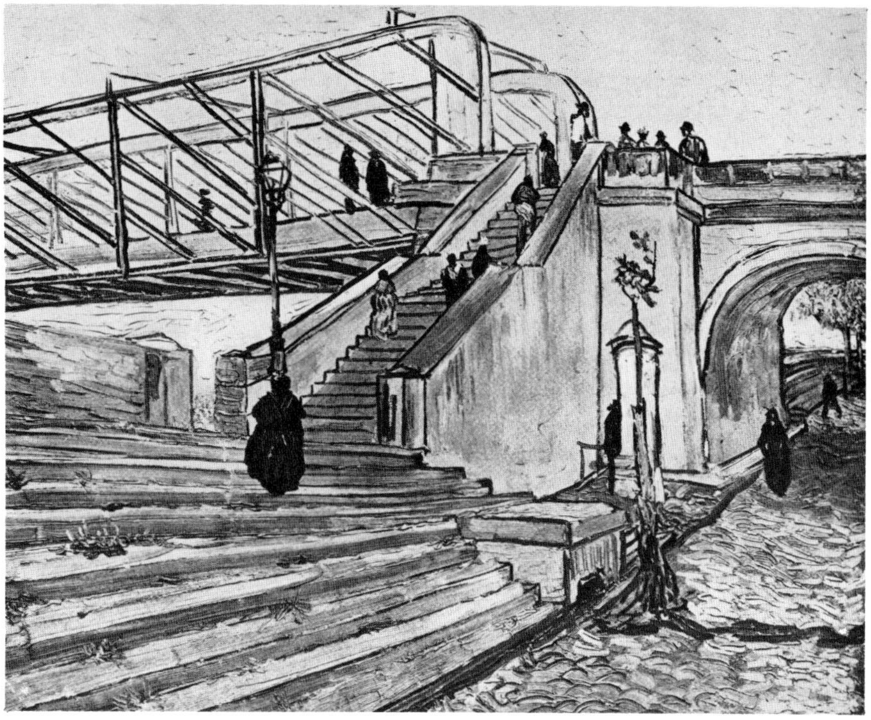

(24) *The Trinquetaille bridge,* **Arles 1888, oil on canvas, 73.5 x 92.5, New York, Private collection.**

(25) *The Trinquetaille bridge.*

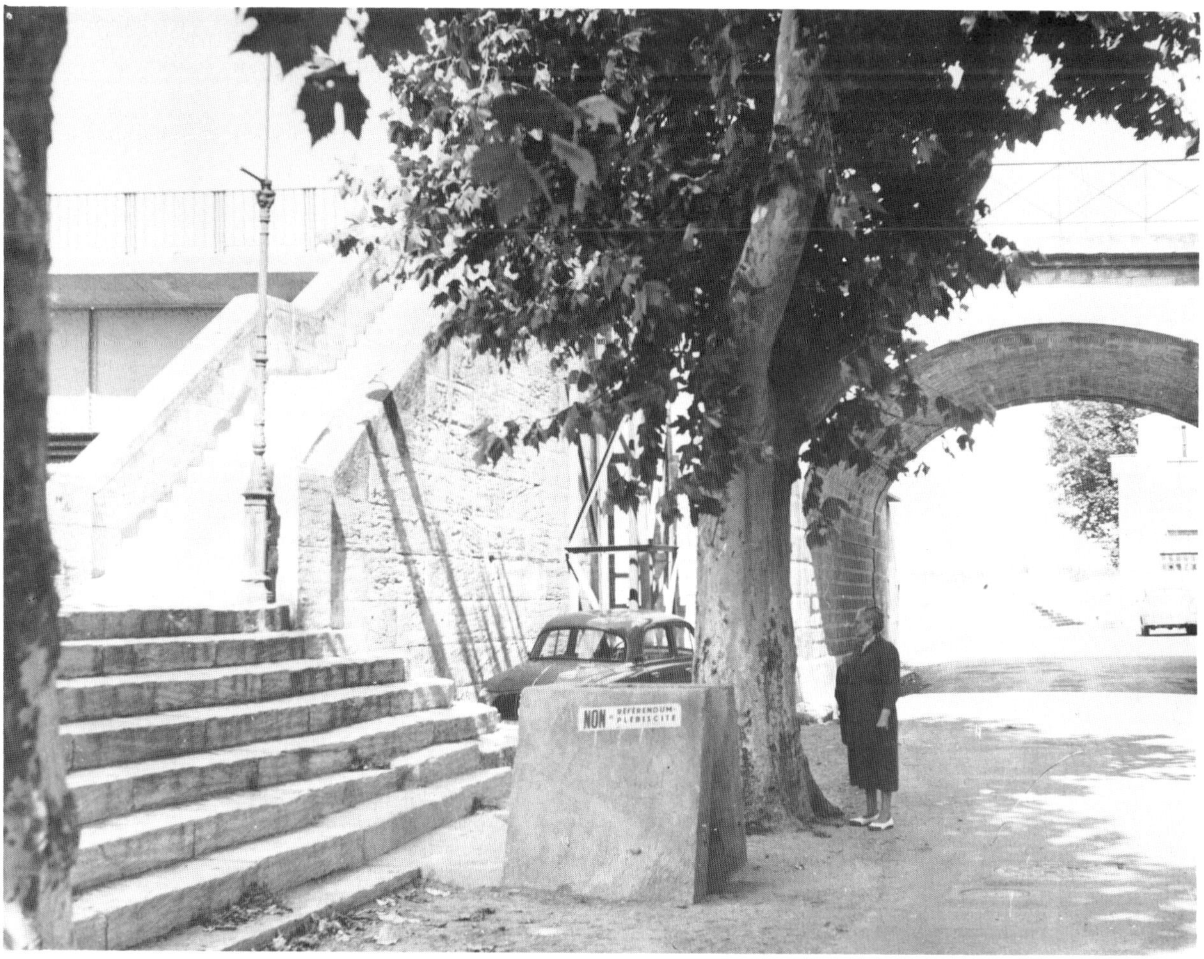

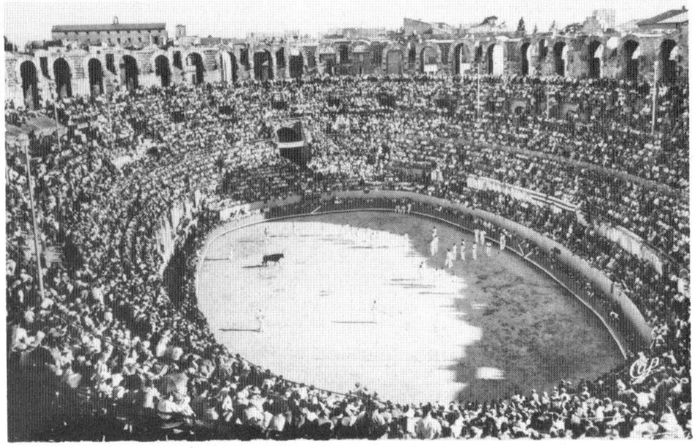

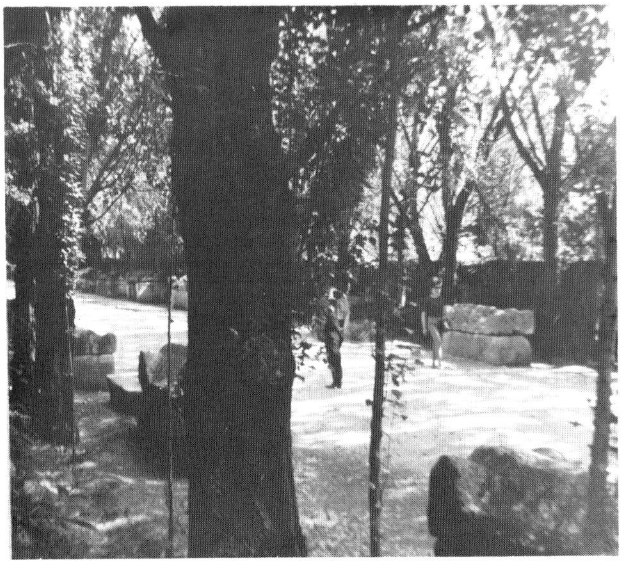

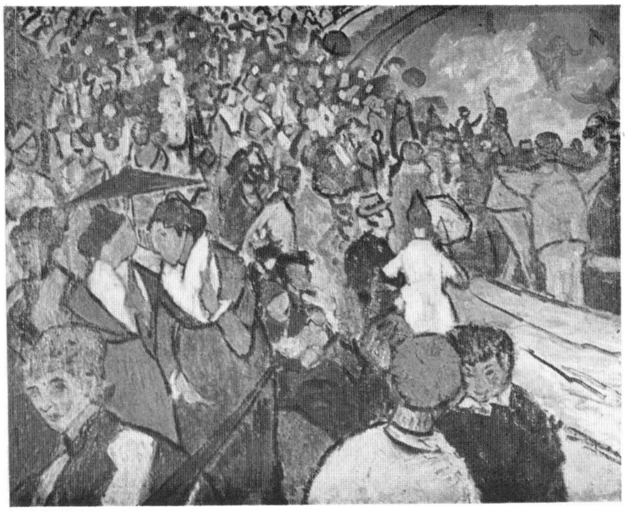

(26) *The Roman amphitheatre at Arles.*

(27) *The spectators in the Arena,* Arles 1888, oil on canvas, 73 x 92 cm, Leningrad, The Hermitage.

(28) *Les Alyscamps, Arles.*

(29) *Les Alyscamps,* Arles 1888, oil on canvas, 73 x 92 cm, Otterlo, Rijksmuseum Kröller-Müller.

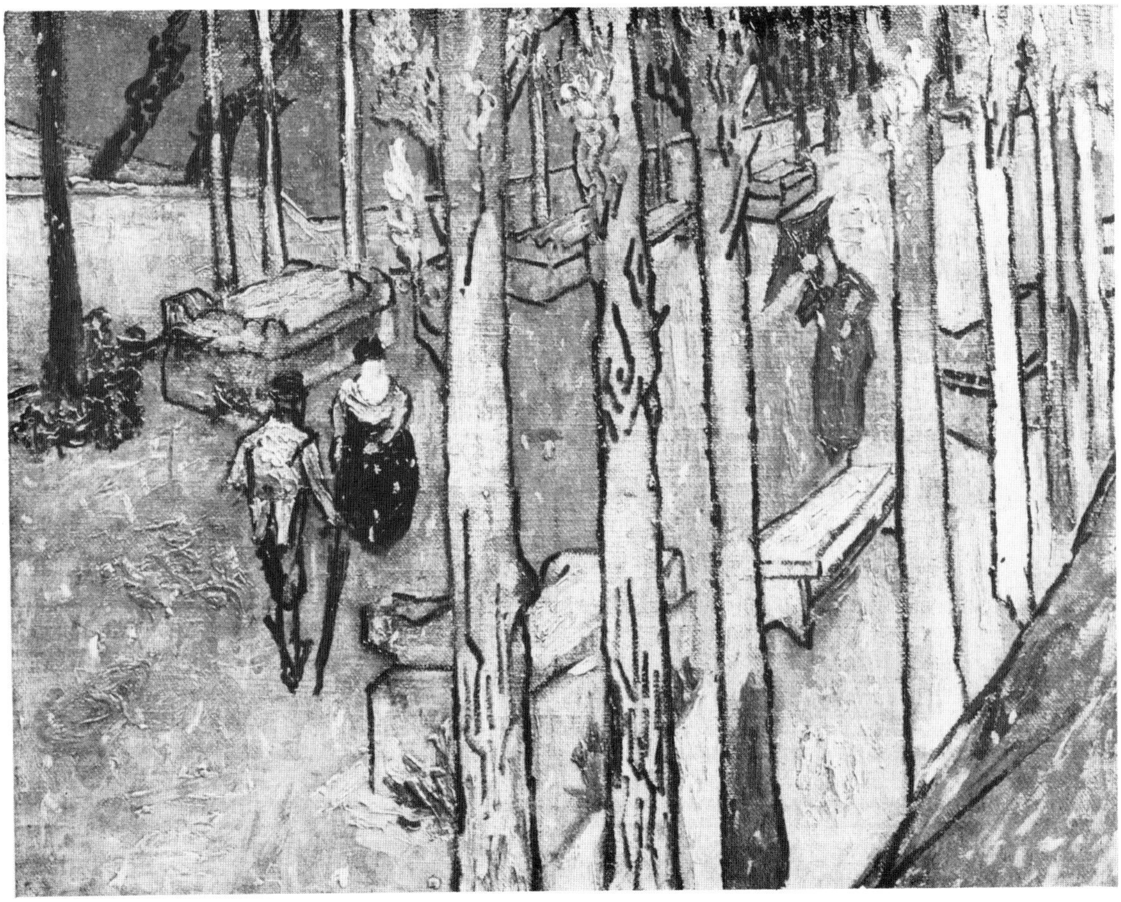

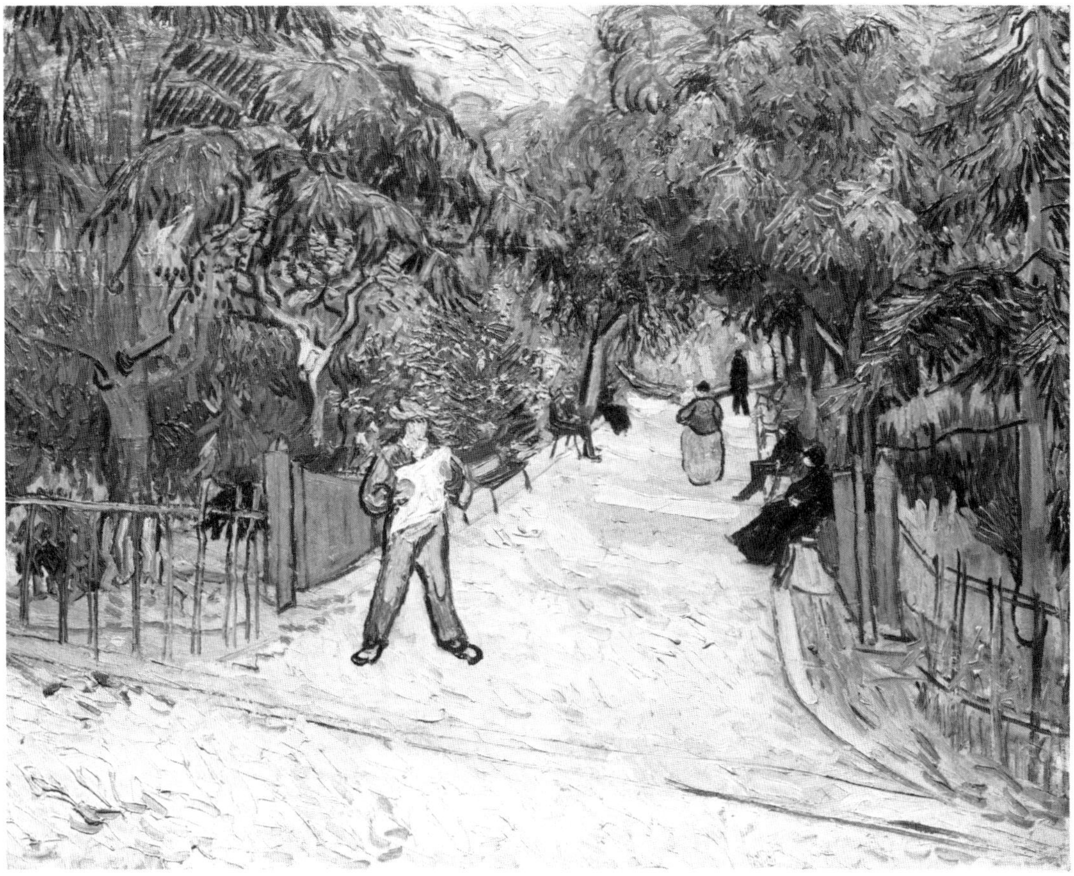

(30) *Man reading newspaper in the public garden,* **Arles 1888, oil on canvas, 72.5 x 91 cm, Washington, The Phillips Collection.**

(31) *The public garden at Arles.*

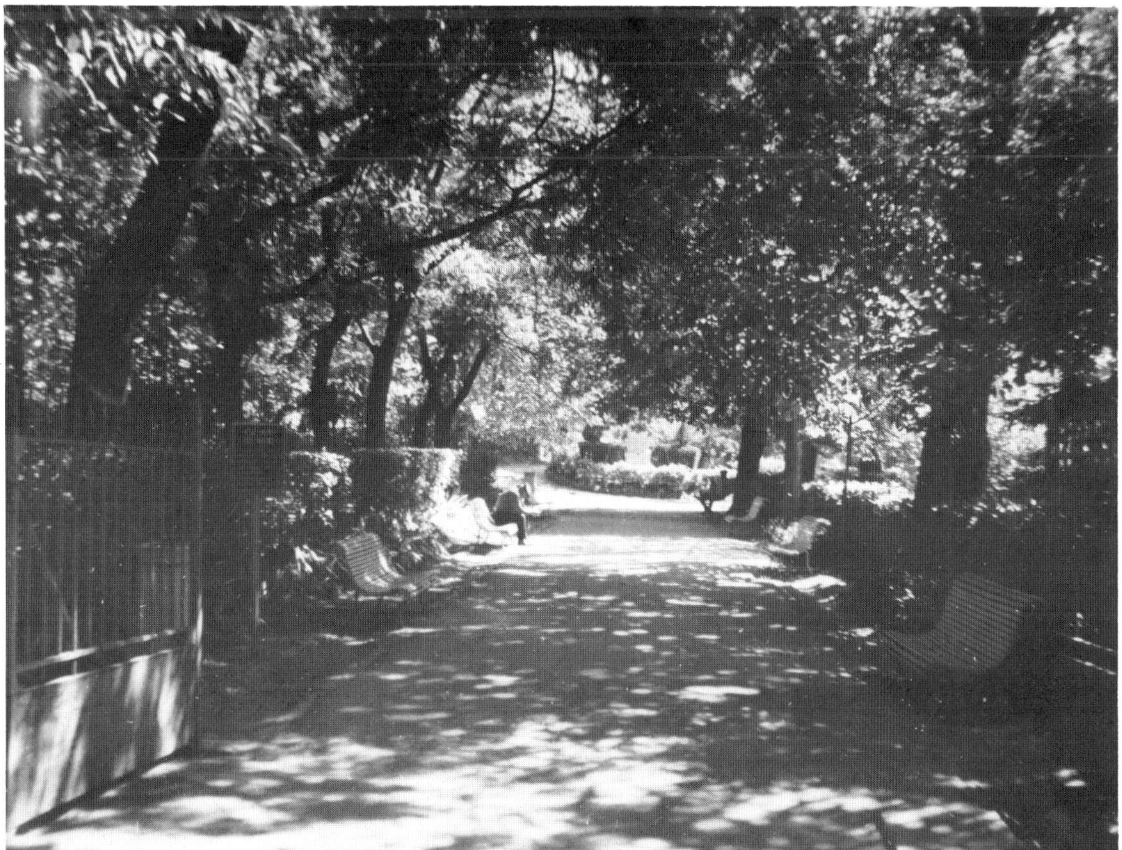

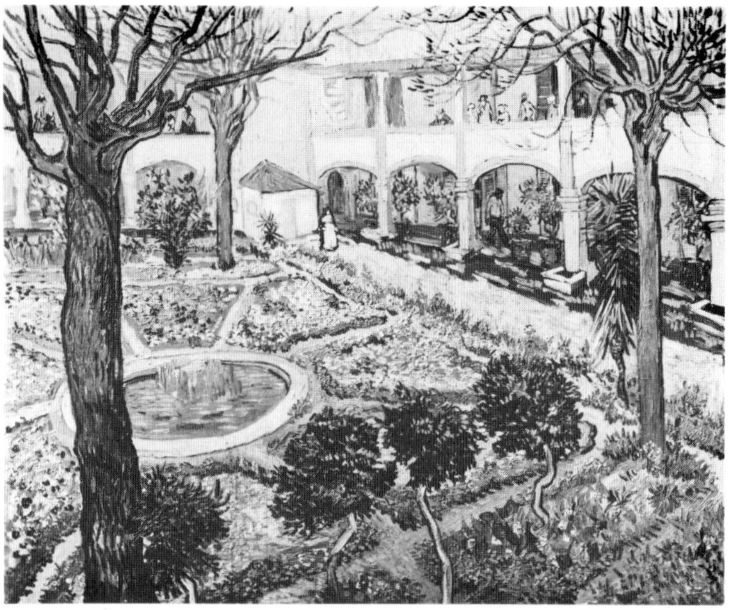

(32) *The courtyard of the hospital in Arles,* **Arles 1889, oil on canvas, 73 x 92 cm, Winterthur, Oskar Reinhart collection.**

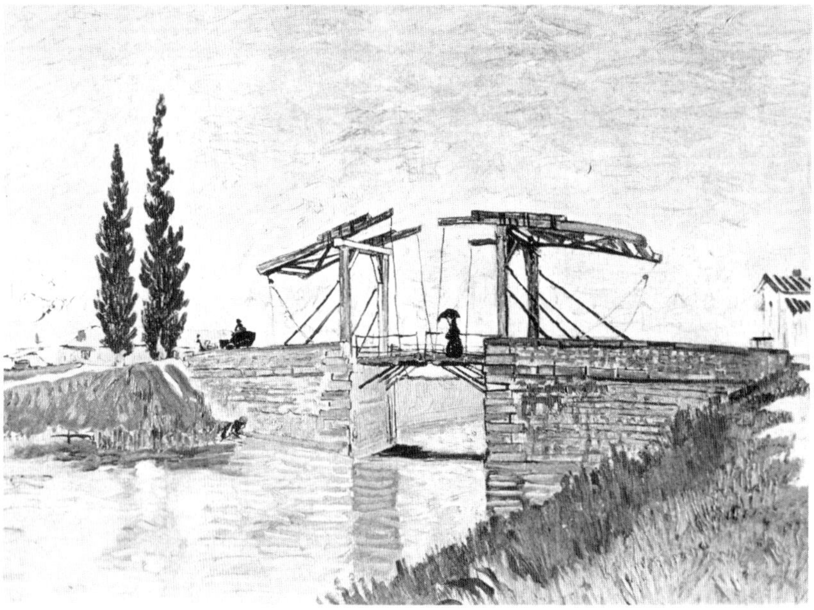

(33) *Drawbridge with Lady with parasol,* Arles 1888, oil on canvas, 49.5 x 64 cm, Cologne, Wallraf-Richartz Museum.

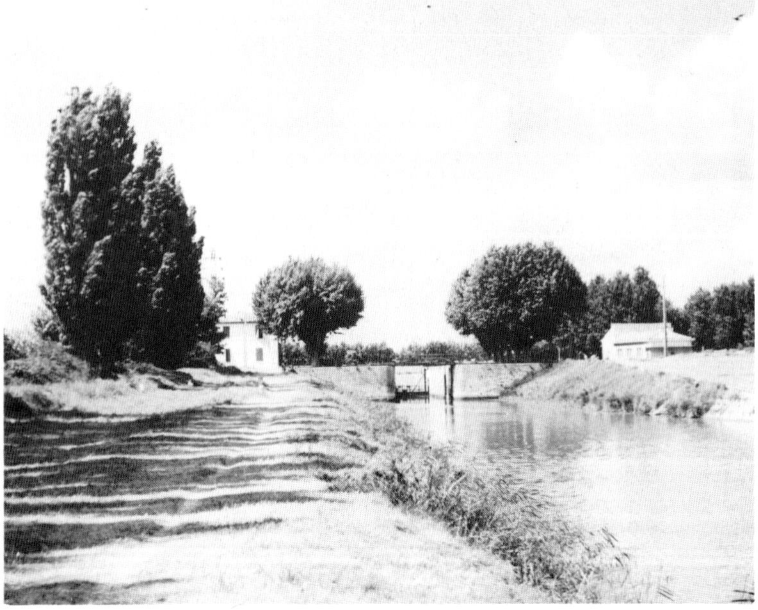

(34) *Bridge across the Arles canal.*

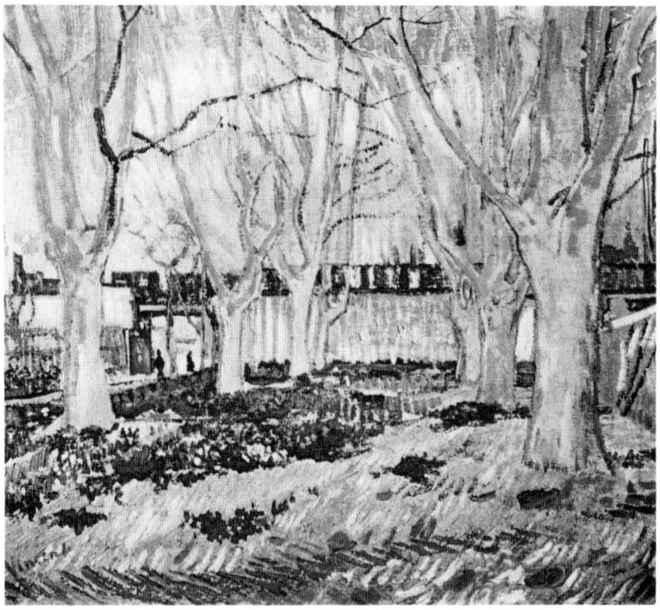

(35) *Lane with plane trees,* **Arles 1888, oil on canvas, 45 x 49 cm, Paris, Musée Rodin.**

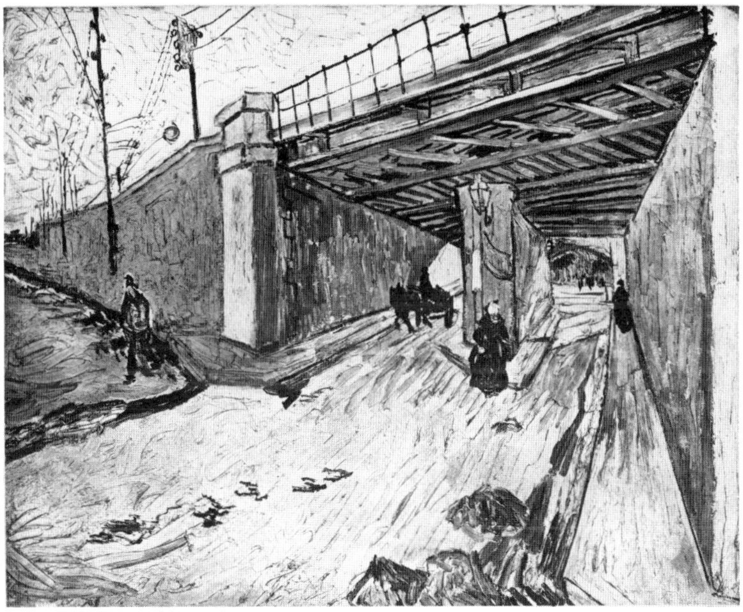

(36) *Railway viaducts,* **Arles 1888, oil on canvas, 71 x 92 cm, Switzerland, Private collection.**

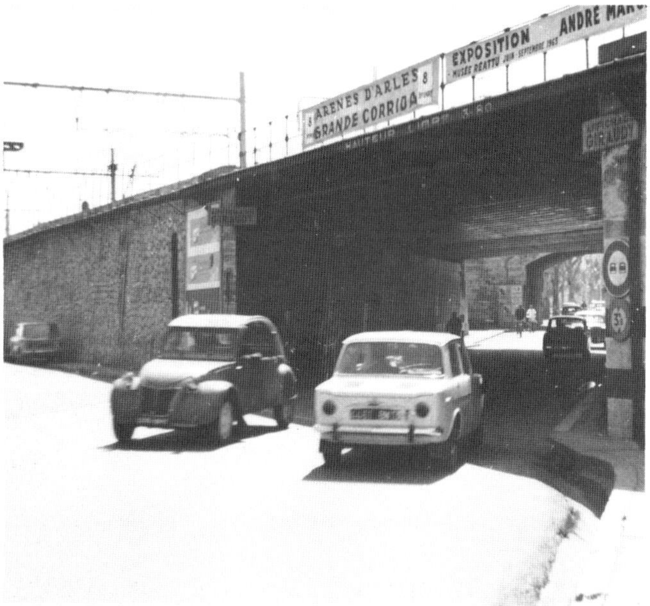

(37) *Railway viaducts.*

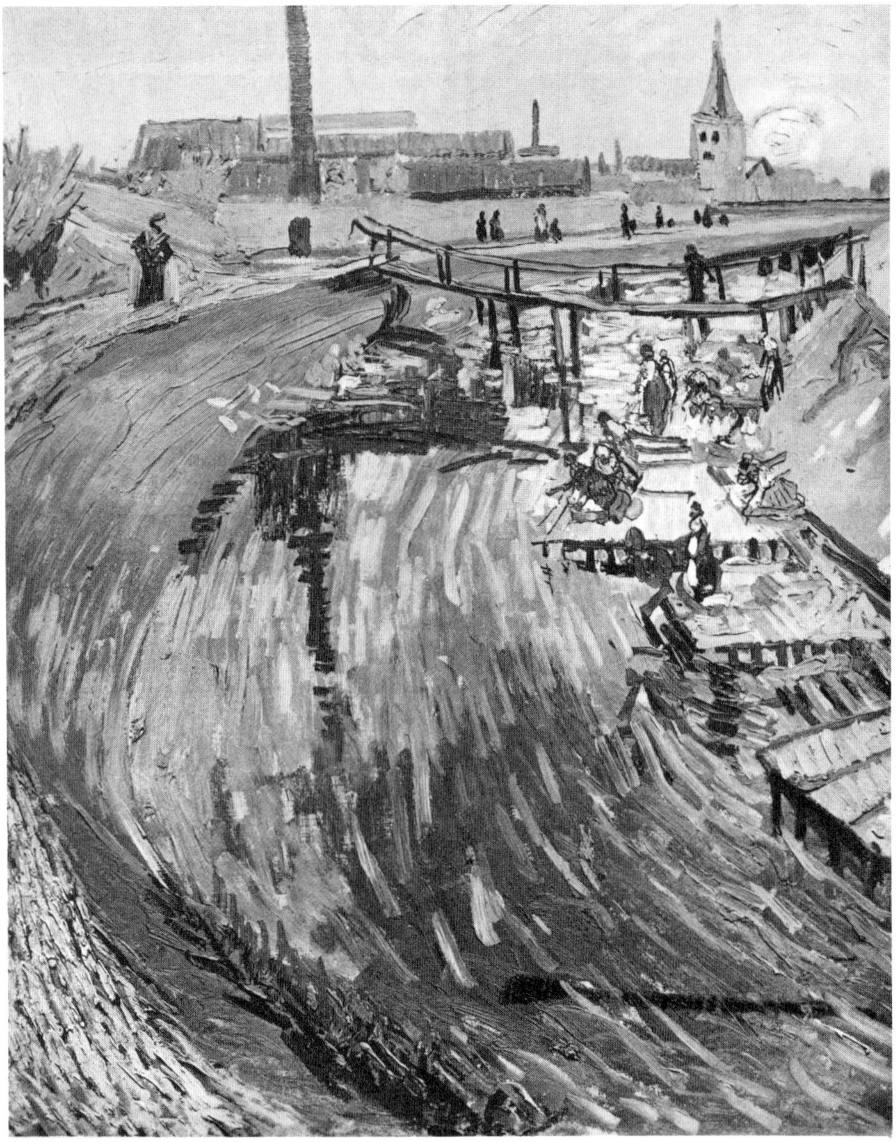

(38) *La Roubine du Roi with women washing,* **Arles 1888, oil on canvas, 74 x 60 cm, New York, Private collection.**

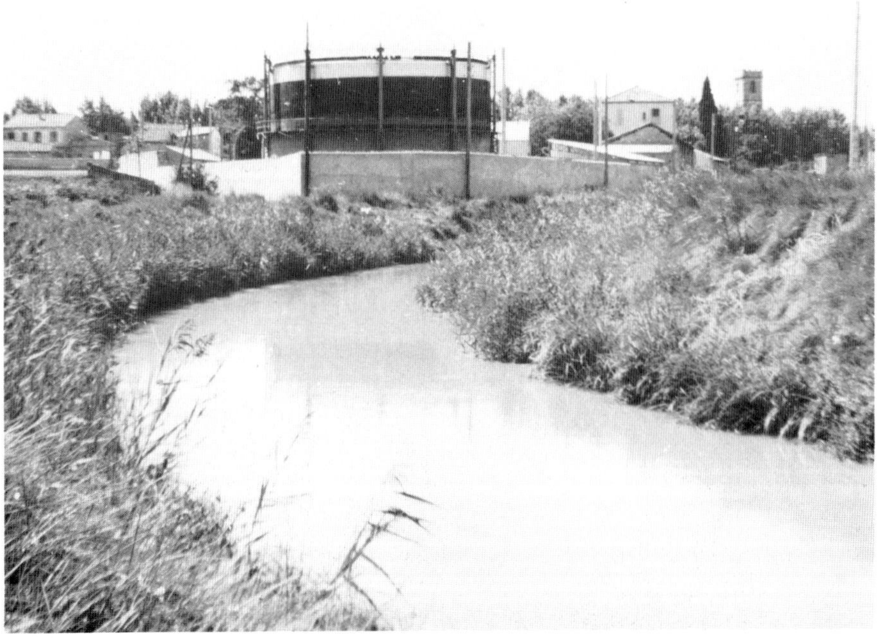

(39) *La Roubine du Roi.*

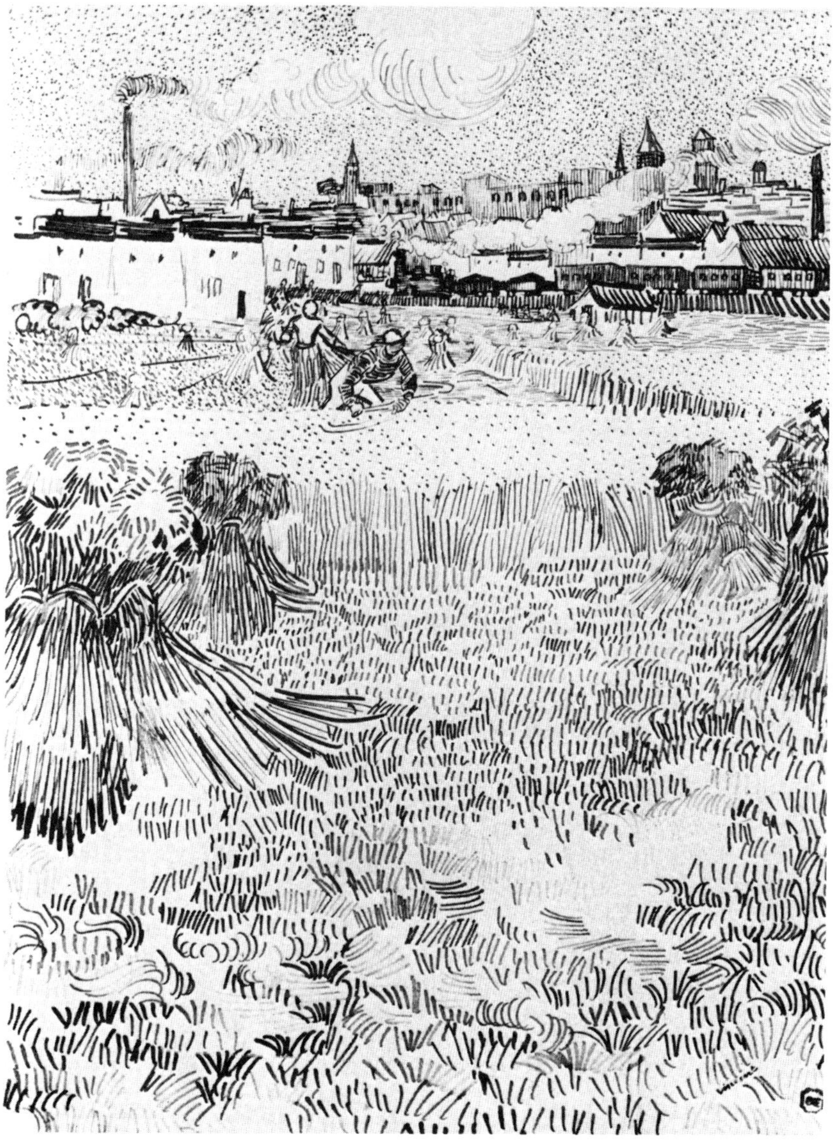

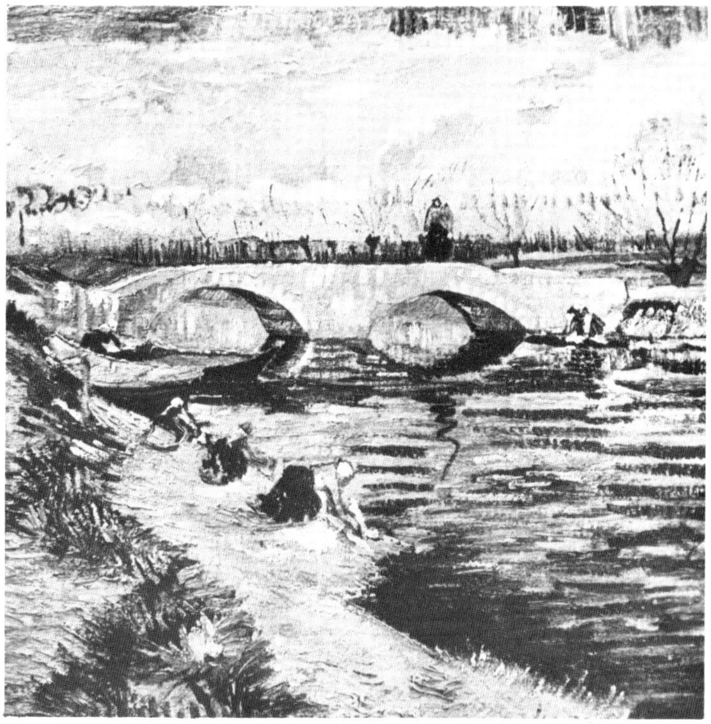

(40) *Wheatfield with sheaves and Arles in background,* **Arles 1888, pen and ink, 31.5 x 24 cm. Location unknown.**

(41) *Landscape with rustic bridge,* **Arles 1888, oil on canvas, 46 x 49 cm, Private collection.**

(42) *Bridge over the Vigueirat canal.*

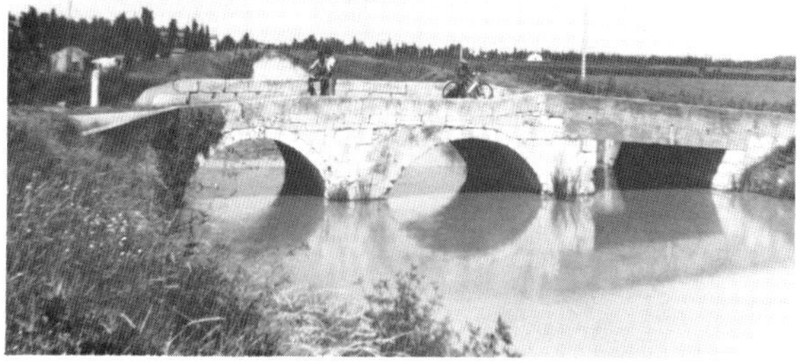

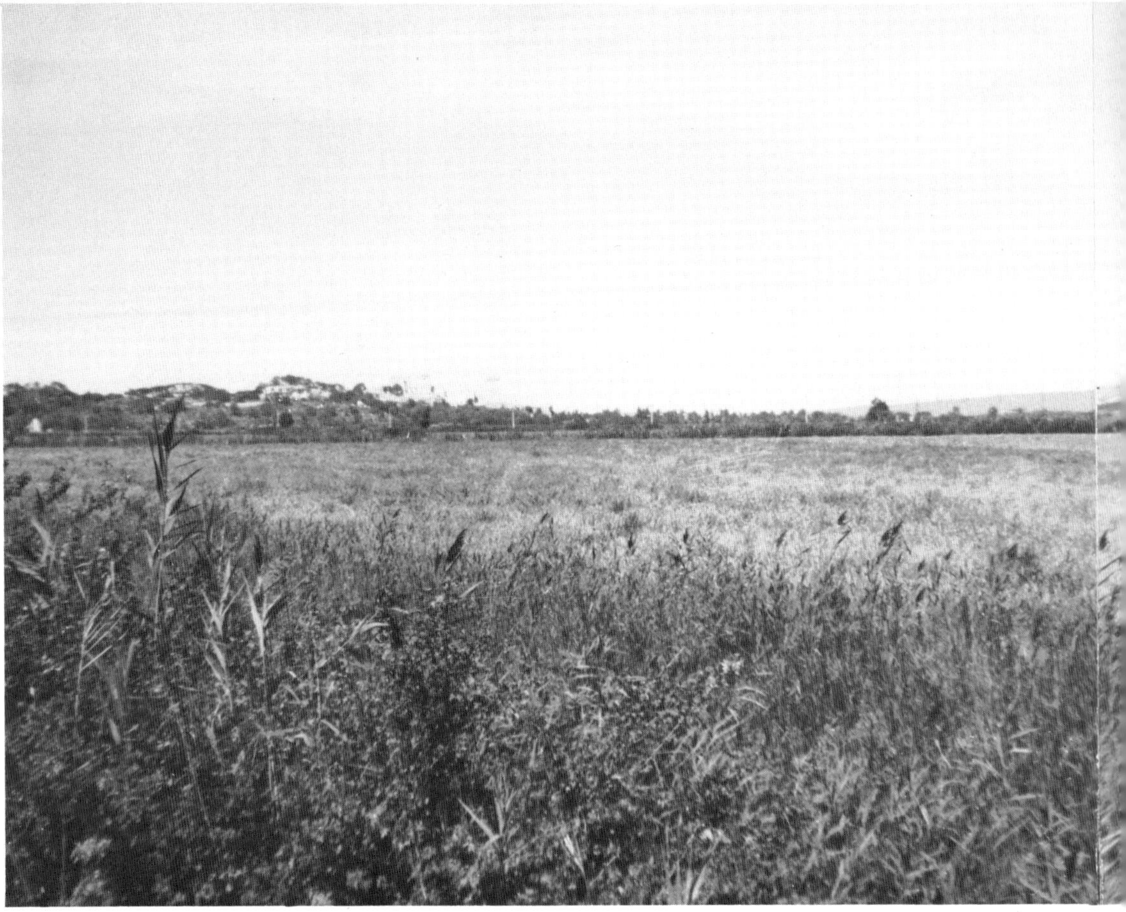

(43) *Photograph of La Crau with the Abbey of Mont Majour and the Mont de Cordes.*

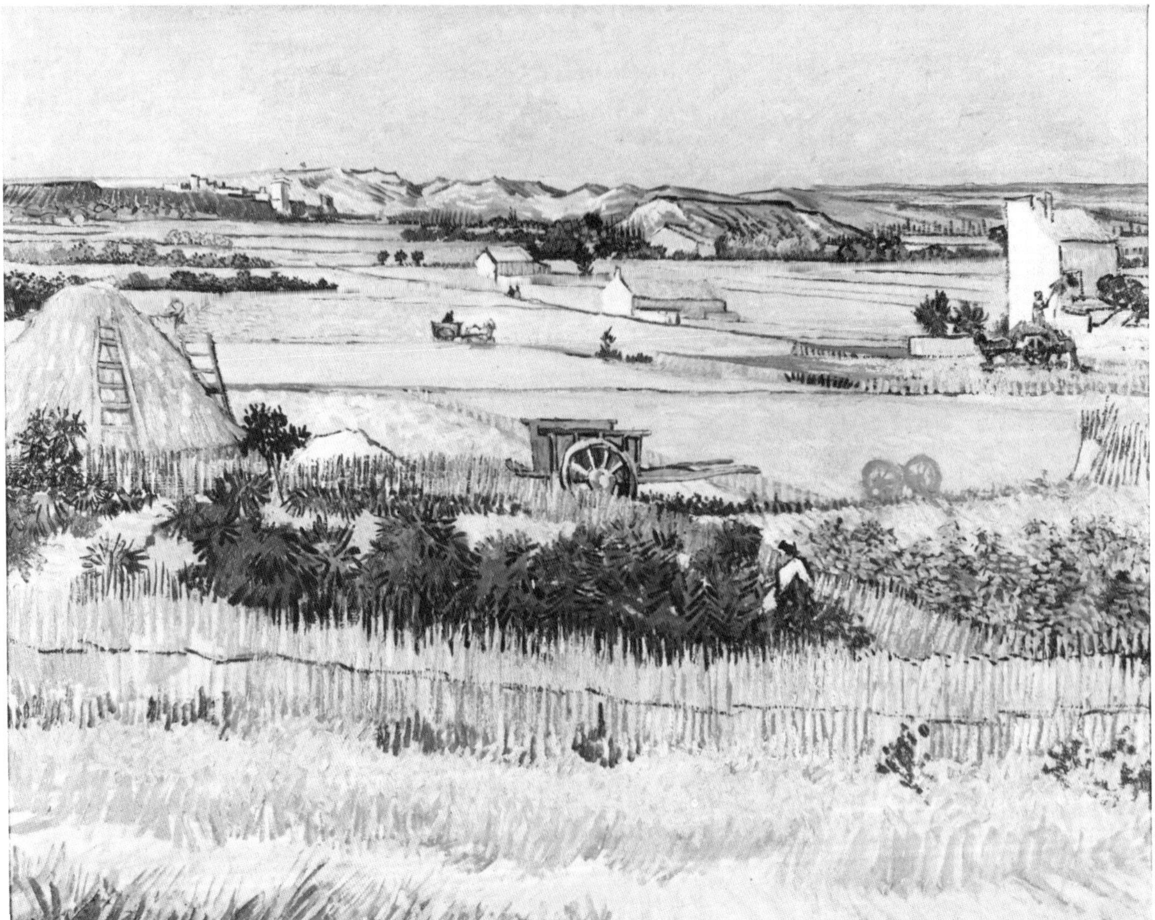

(44) *Harvest,* Arles 1888, oil on canvas, 72.5 x 92 cm, Amsterdam, Rijksmuseum Vincent van Gogh.

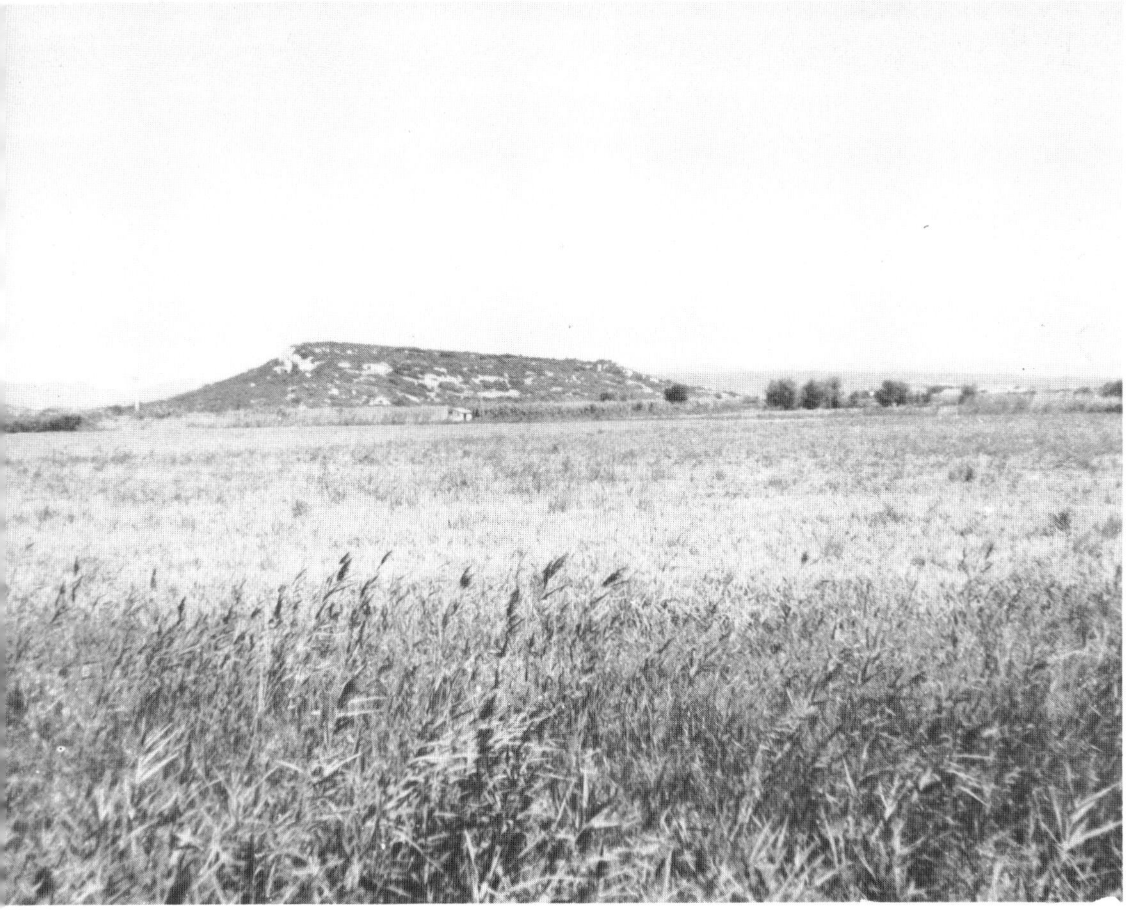

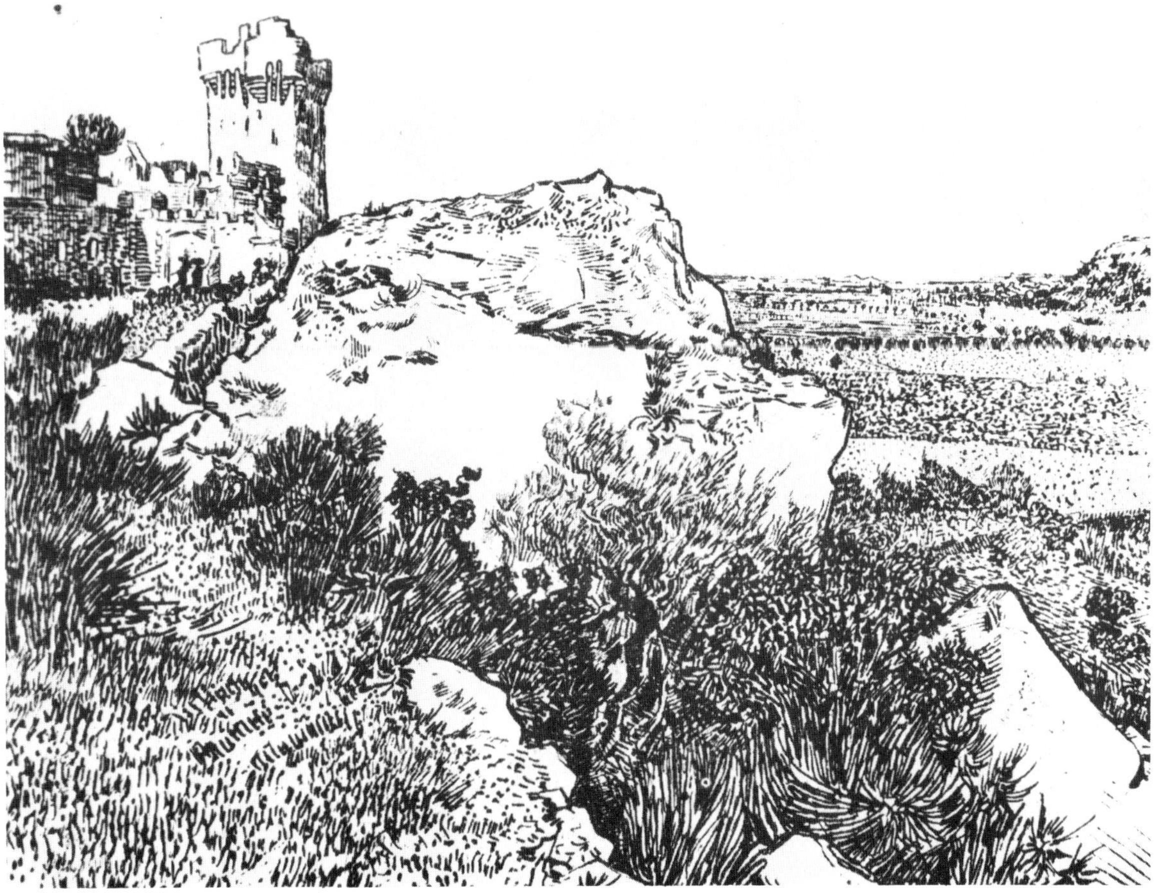

(45) *Hill with ruins of Mont Majour*, **Arles 1888, pen and ink, 47.5 x 59 cm, Amsterdam, Riksmuseum (Rijksprentenkabinet).**

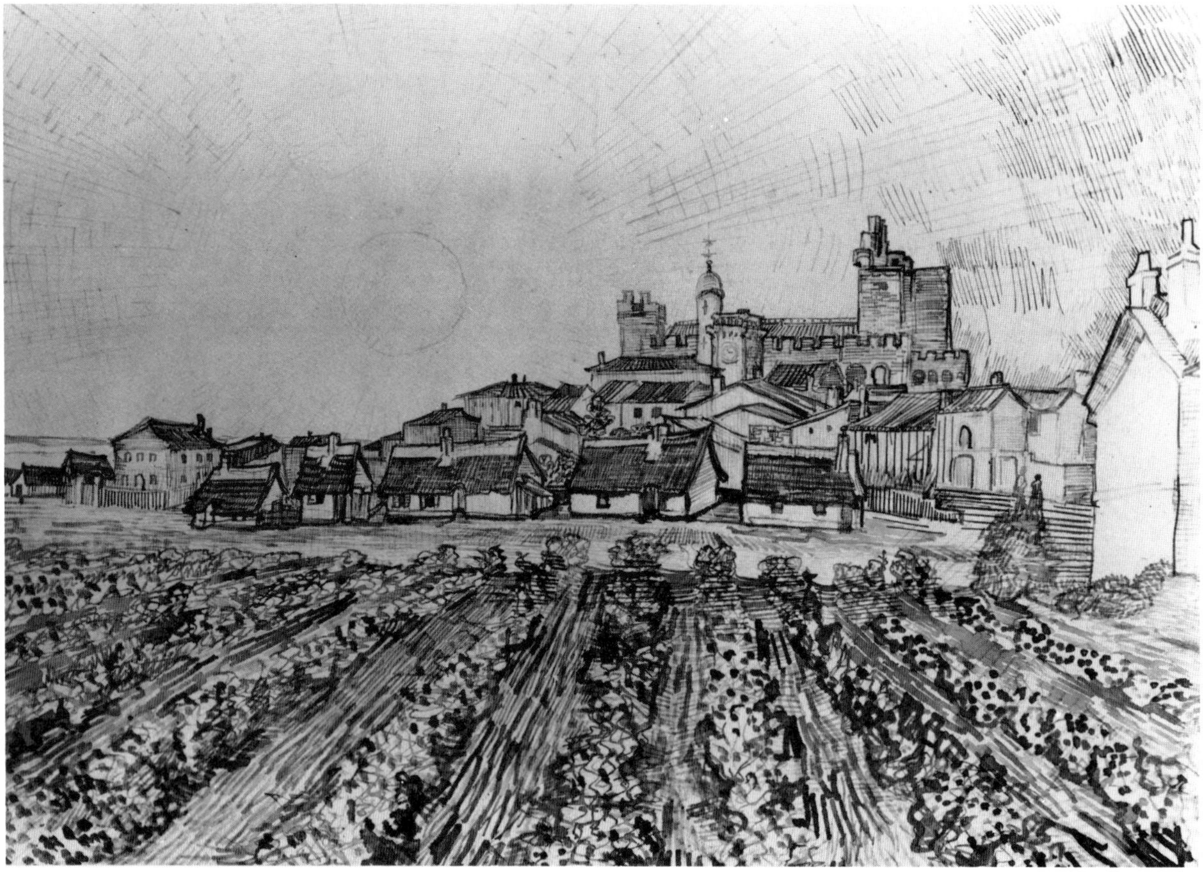

(46) *View of Saintes Maries,* **Arles 1888, pen and ink, 43 x 60 cm, Winterthur, Oskar Reinhardt Collection.**

(47) *Church at Saintes Maries.*

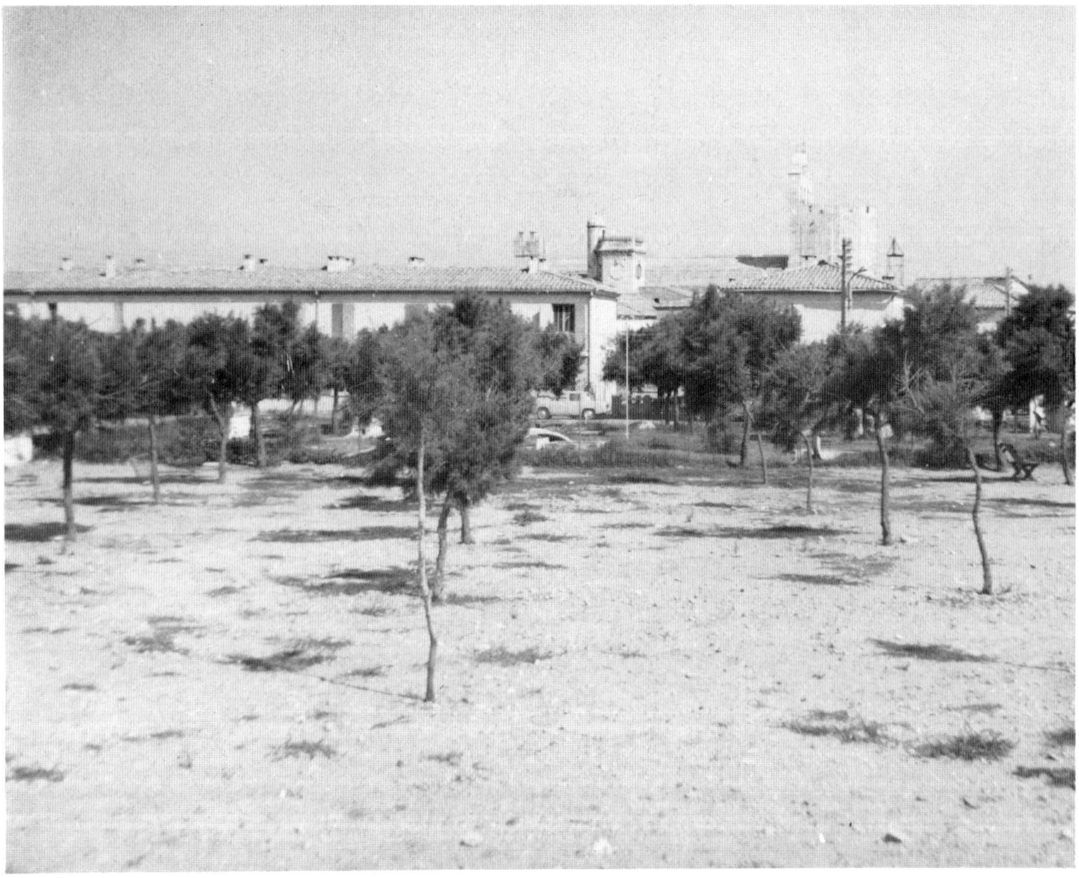

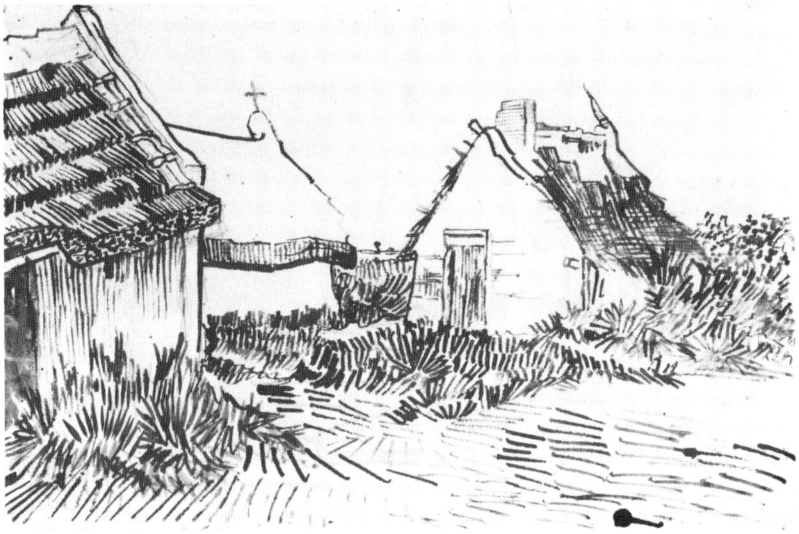

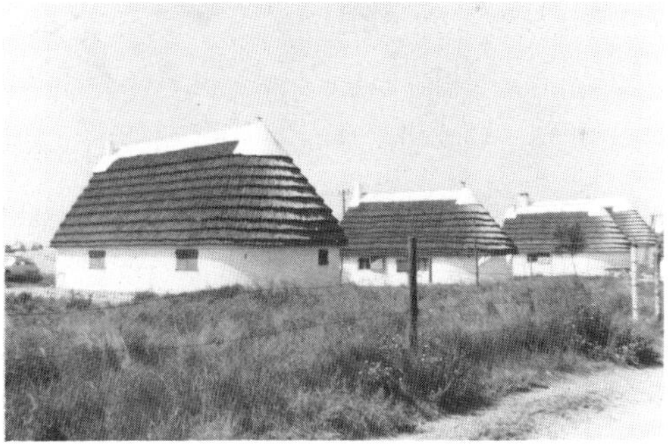

(49) *Cottages at Saintes Maries.*

(48) *Three cottages at Saintes Maries,* **Arles 1888, pencil, pen and ink, 30 x 47 cm, Amsterdam, Rijksmuseum Vincent van Gogh.**

(50) *Trees in front of the entrance to the asylum,* **St Rémy 1889, 90 x 71 cm, Los Angeles, The Armand Hammer Foundation.**

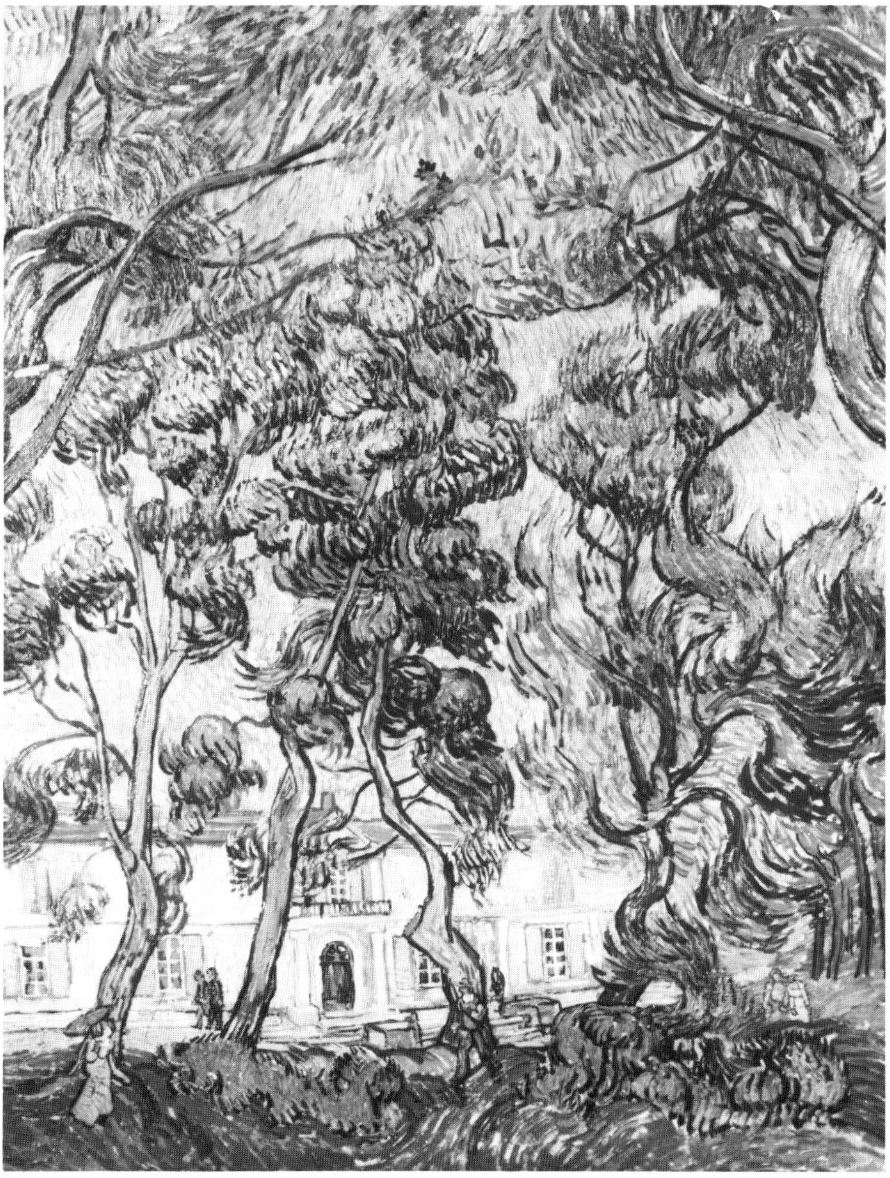

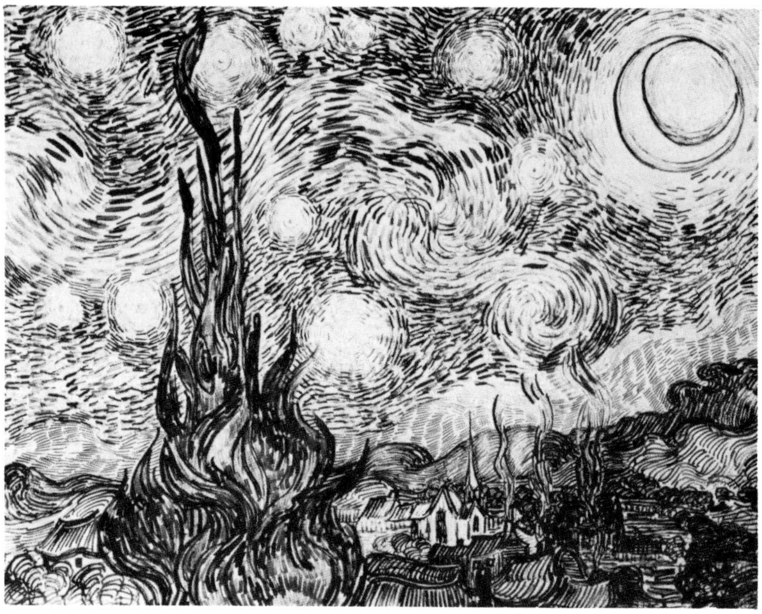

(51) *The starry night,* St Rémy 1889, pen and ink, 47 x 62.5 cm, destroyed (formerly Bremen Kunsthalle).

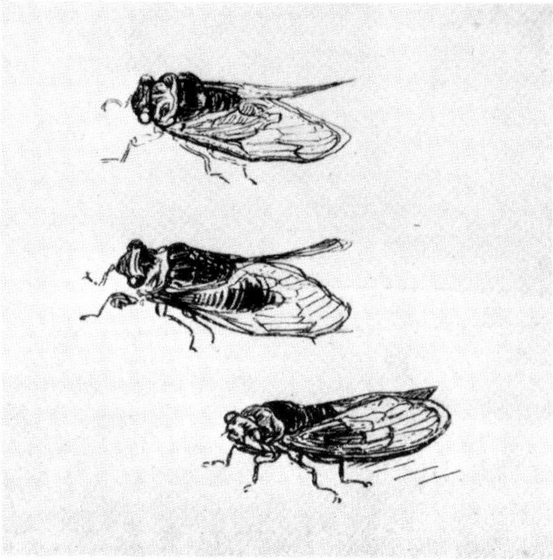

(52) *Three cicadas,* St Rémy 1889, pen and ink, sketch in letter 603 to Theo 20.5 x 18cm. Amsterdam, Rijksmuseum Vincent van Gogh.

(53) *Entrance to a quarry,* St Rémy 1889, oil on canvas, 52 x 64 cm, location unknown.

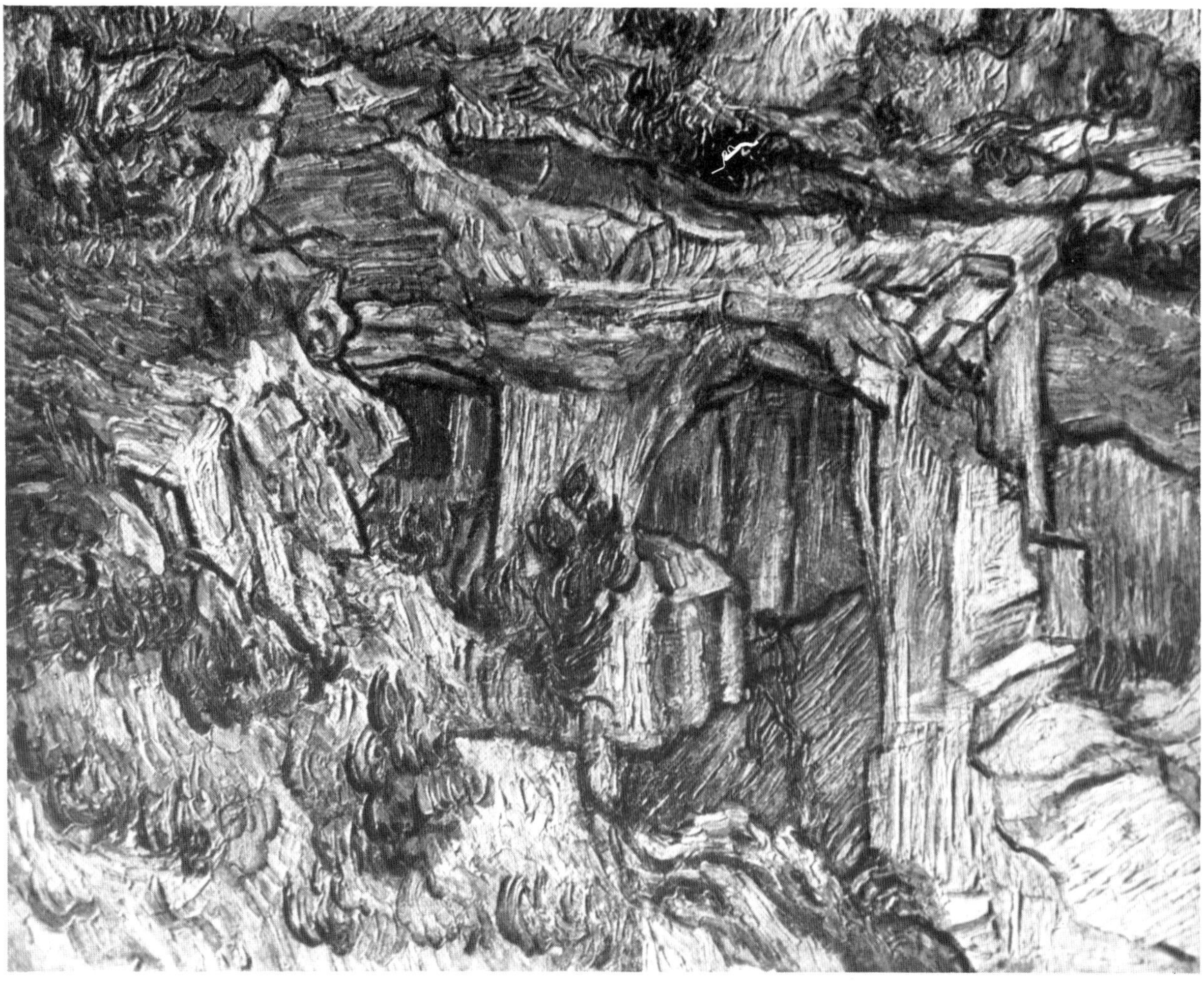

THE VAN GOGH INDUSTRY

"Van Gogh is not Van Gogh now. Society has sterilised him in its laboratory, he has been vulgarised as part of its encyclopedic material, he has been retailed in samples in its salerooms, splendid houses and official buildings".[1] These remarks by Jean Cassou occur in an essay concerning the exploitation of art in bourgeois, consumer societies. Cassou cites Van Gogh merely as an example of his general thesis but it may be instructive to examine the case of Van Gogh in greater depth. I shall not be directly concerned with Van Gogh's oeuvre or his importance as one of the founders of modern art; what I shall discuss is the way his work, and life, have been turned into a commodity, packaged and marketed for popular consumption via a variety of media, in the period since his death in 1890; hence the expression *'Van Gogh industry'*.[2]

The primary source materials of this industry are those artifacts directly produced by the mental and physical labour of the artist, in this instance Van Gogh's paintings, drawings and letters. Year by year since 1890 his fame has spread and the demand for his work has grown until now it commands huge sums in the salerooms: in February 1970 Vincent's canvas *'Le cypres et l'abre en fleurs'* was sold to a mystery buyer (in fact Aristotle Onassis) for $1,300,000 (£541,670) the highest price yet paid for a Van Gogh. The American magazine *Auction* a journal for collectors and investors in art, described the sale as a *"black tie event"* and issued a plastic disc recording the bidding to provide a permanent record of the *"dramatic tension of that memorable evening"*! It also carried an article on an American businessman who had made the second highest bid.[3]

The existing stock of Vincent's work available for sale progressively decreases as items enter the permanent collections of the world's major galleries and museums. (This stock was already severely restricted by the fact that a large proportion of Van Gogh's output belonged to Vincent's nephew Dr. V. W. Van Gogh) thus scarcity value is increasingly reflected in auction prices. Of course, there is one illicit method of overcoming the problem of the shortage of primary materials and that is to invent them: to manufacture spurious Van Goghs. So lucrative were the rewards in the Van Gogh industry during the period of Vincent's posthumous rise to fame – a period when his oeuvre was only partially documented – that he attracted the attentions of several forgers and crooked dealers: the latest edition of J. B. de la Faille's catalogue raisonné illustrates over sixty examples of these forgeries.[4] In turn these forgeries provided a number of experts and connoisseurs with the legitimate work of authenticating 'Van Gogh' paintings.

Curiously akin to forgery are those re-creations of Van Gogh's works produced by reputable artists of later generations out of a profound admiration of his life and work. English artists in particular seem to find a special inspiration in Van Gogh. I am thinking of Francis Bacon, Derrick Greaves, Clive Barker, David Pearson and also the Australian-born artist Martin Sharp. These artists have not merely been influenced by Vincent's vivid colour or his violent brushwork – as were the Fauves and the Expressionists – rather they have attempted to re-create his images in the way that a medium at a seance tries to conjure up the voice and spirit of a departed soul.

For example,in 1967 Greaves produced a series of paintings, drawings and screenprints entitled *'Homage to Van Gogh'*. He created them after making a pilgrimage to see Vincent's motifs in Provence, a journey on which he had taken a copy of Vincent's letters. Greaves' paintings explore Van Gogh's sower theme and directly utilise his images – sun, hand, birds, seed – though Greaves simplifies and enlarges them. In a statement describing his Homage series Greaves talks of his *"long standing debt"* to Van Gogh and calls him *"Guru Vincent"*.[5]

Francis Bacon's interest in Van Gogh is well known. Bacon's one man show at the Hanover Gallery, London in 1957 was largely devoted to Van Gogh inspired paintings. According to John Russell the link between the two artists is a concern with *"meaningful distortion"*.[6] While hints of Van Gogh's mental breakdown can be detected in some paintings of the Arles period at the same time there are many extremely serene and harmonious canvases which strike one as the productions of a perfectly lucid consciousness, therefore Bacon's neurotic and anxiety-ridden figure of Vincent on the road to Tarascon is a somewhat one-sided characterisation and reveals more about Bacon than it does about Van Gogh's state of mind.

Clive Barker has extended Van Gogh's oeuvre into another dimension and medium: he has created 'Van Gogh sculpture'; i.e., three-dimensional, chromium-plated metal representations of objects depicted in certain of Vincent's canvases, for example *'Still life with drawing board', 'Sunflowers'* and *'Vincent's chair'.*[7] Another British artist who has produced Van Gogh sculpture – in the form of environmental constructions – is David Pearson. Adrian Henri describes him as *"an obsessional artist from Lancashire"* and adds *"His work is almost entirely motivated by the life and work of Van Gogh, the most striking pieces being larger-than-life tableaux based on* **'The potato eaters'**, **'The cornfield'** *and* **'Van Gogh's bedroom'**.[8]

Martin Sharp, the *Oz* magazine illustrator and graphic artist, has devised a series of collages called 'artoons' which make use of numerous images derived from Van Gogh's paintings. Sharp's *Artbook* consists entirely of piquant juxtapositions of iconography clipped from reproductions of works by different artists.[9] Van Gogh, for example, is paired with Roy Lichtenstein, René Magritte, Giorgio de Chirico, Pierre Bonnard, Edvard Munch, Paul Cézanne, Edgar Degas, Andy Warhol and, most incestuously of all, Francis Bacon. In spite of the obvious sardonic humour of Sharp's collages the homage to Van Gogh manifests itself in the frequency with which Sharp employs Vincent's images. Sharp has also produced a poster eulogising Van Gogh and paintings in which the figure of Vincent on the road to Tarascon is pursued by Mickey Mouse. (What Mickey and Vincent have in common, apart from fame and ears, is difficult to imagine.) Sharp's artoons were pre-dated by those of an American graphic artist called Ward Kimball. In his book *Art Afterpieces* Kimball subjects reproductions of sixty famous oil paintings to a host of indignities.[10] The book contains two amended Van Gogh's; one shows Vincent's Sunflowers in a pot labelled 'VAT 69' and the second illustrates one of the drawbridge-over-the-canal series in which a huge ocean going liner is about to demolish the drawbridge.

The existence on the one hand of an avid interest in Van Gogh among the art loving public and on the other an extremely limited supply of primary artifacts to satisfy the demands for information, and the desire to possess examples of his images, has inevitably led to the development of a host of secondary products loosely based on the primary materials or supportive to them: art histories, picture books, biographies, collections of photographs of motifs, calendars, poems, plays, films, TV documentaries, a song, posters, and reproductions of all sizes and qualities. Let us consider these spin-off products in more detail.

Academic by-products are legion. An up-to-date bibliography of writings on Van Gogh – catalogues, periodical articles and books – would include well over one thousand separate items. Marc Edo Tralbaut, a Dutch art historian, spent his life collecting literature and relics relating to Vincent and himself contributed seventy-three essays to the Van Gogh archive. Tralbaut's collection has been left to the Netherlands State Van Gogh Museum and in the same country a Vincent Van Gogh Foundation exists to sustain further research. In 1972 a Van Gogh Society was formed in Cambridge, England and already claims a membership of sixty to seventy.[11] A quarterly journal, entitled *Vincent*, exclusively devoted to Van Gogh's oeuvre has been published in Holland since 1970.

The artist is now so fully documented that one might think that no further comment is possible. However Vincent suffered from a mysterious mental aberration; its exact nature has puzzled many psychologists and psychiatrists in the past and since Vincent cannot be resurrected to undergo modern medical tests his illness continues to provide a plausible pretext for academic speculation.

The publishing industries of many countries have reason to be grateful to Van Gogh. Vincent's letters to his brother Theo, to his other relatives and to his colleagues are unsurpassed as a record of his life. The originals are also prized on aesthetic grounds because of the many drawings and sketches they contain. However, the originals do not concern us here so much as the published translations, which are available in English in three large volumes at a cost of £24 the set. Even his most devoted admirers must be daunted by the cost and the sheer mass of material – the first two volumes are especially heavy going – so publishers have been quick to provide more digestible selections, packaged for undemanding consumption. One recent selection describes itself as Van Gogh's *"diary"*. Often publishers employ a celebrity to act as editor, for example the late W. H. Auden, in order to add a touch more glamour.

The letters have provided source material for many biographies of Van Gogh. The more popular and fictionalised of these works concentrate on his personal relationships rather than his art. Stuart Hall and Paddy Whannel quote the following words from the paperback edition of Irving Stone's *Lust for Life*:

He didn't kiss – he crushed!
He didn't propose – he demanded!
He was not just a man, he was a lover
With a consuming LUST FOR LIFE[12]

The trouble with these fictionalised biographies, as John Berger points out, is that they romanticise failure; they separate the artist's life from the work that makes him great and as a result *"his greatness ... invests with false significance ... his loneliness, his temperament, his separation from other people, his personal tragedies."*[13]

The following extracts from two poems by Robert Witz illustrates this romanticism in action:

Van Gogh was alone so he went
To woman, the scarlet mystery.
Through thickening alleyways he bent
His chill, apart, to cut the misery
Of his cold soul . . .

But he, beneath cold sheets had thought
Only of his loneliness, his soul's chill, so
Alone. The desert of his life was expanding:
The shudder of bandage and head, his ear and Gauguin
Gone, even the jeers of the people swelling
Like a sore beneath his window, gone . . .

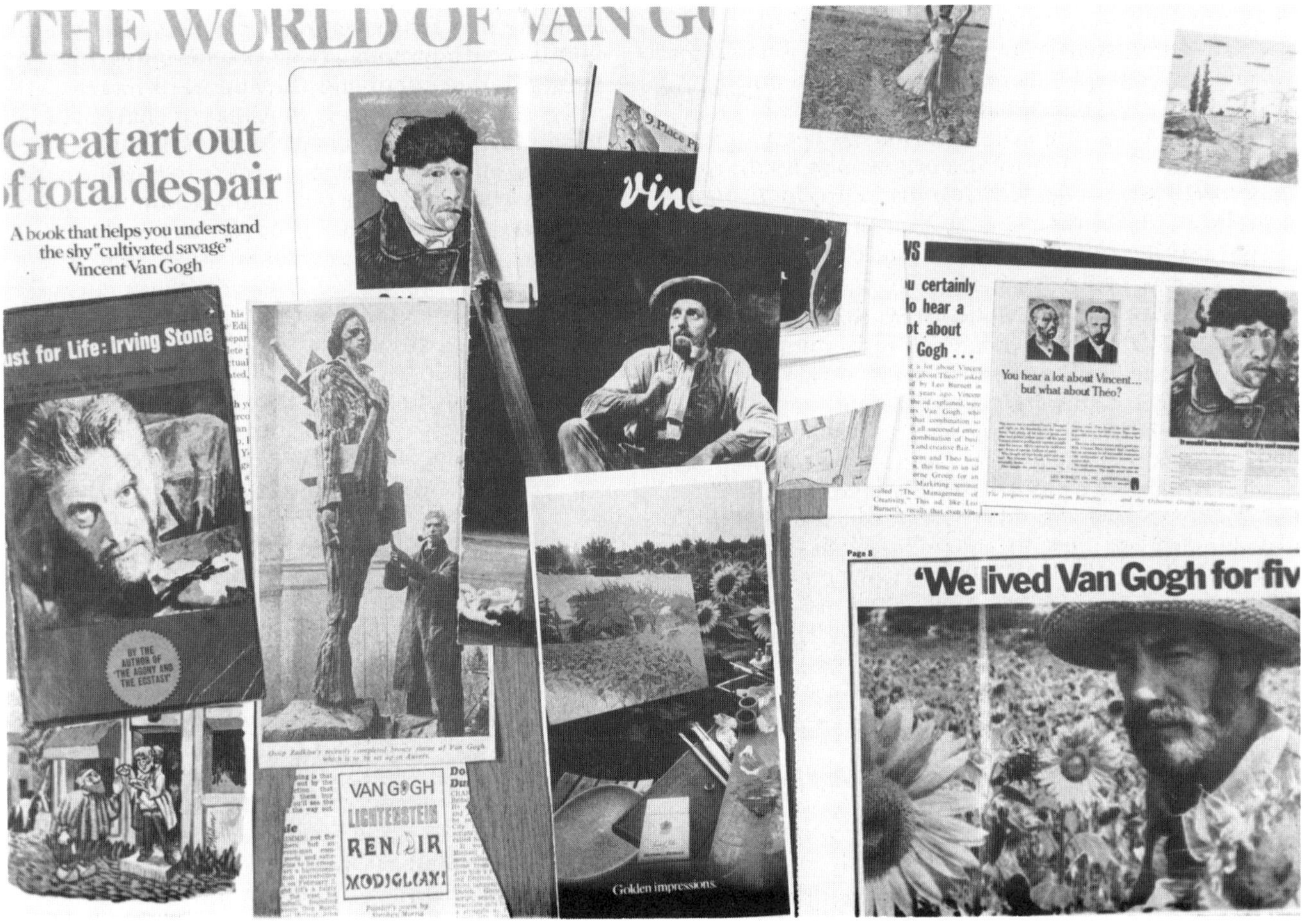

(54) *Images from the van Gogh industry (1)*

It is doubly disappointing to find these poems published in a journal with high social ideals.[14]

Irving Stone's *Lust for Life* spawned the film of the book starring Kirk Douglas as Van Gogh and Anthony Quinn – the all-purpose foreigner of Hollywood – as Gauguin. The film was made in 1956 and directed by Vincente Minnelli. John Berger contends that all these dramatisations, however sincere in intention, present Van Gogh as the problem-child cum gangster, the outsider-criminal and *"just as Van Gogh's temperament is separated from his work so it is also separated from his social environment . . . there is no hint that in many cases he was misunderstood because he saw . . . the hypocritical contradictions of his society and refused to accept them".* Berger's conclusion is that the heroic legend of Van Gogh is *"made in the image of our most destructive and anti-social fantasies".*[15]

It is a sign of the continued potency of the Van Gogh legend that it has inspired one of the top twenty tunes of 1972, namely Don Maclean's *Vincent* issued by United Artists Records:

Starry, starry night
Paint your palette blue and grey
Look out on a summers day
With eyes that know the darkness in my soul
Shadows on the hills
Sketch the trees and the daffodils
Catch the breeze and the winter chills
In colours on the snowy-linen land
Now I understand
What you tried to say to me
How you suffered for your sanity
And how you tried to set them free
They would not listen, they did not know how
Perhaps they'll listen now
Starry, starry night
Flaming flowers that brightly blaze
Swirling clouds in voilet haze
Reflecting Vincent's eyes of china blue . . . etc.

On October 28, 1972 several million viewers watching London Weekend television were introduced to Van Gogh as a light entertainment feature on the Rolf Harris show. Harris, an Australian variety artist who often paints as part of his routine, sketched a four feet high portrait head of Vincent, based on one of Van Gogh's own self-portraits, and as he worked he gave the audience and viewers at home a few of the more lurid facts about Vincent's life. When Harris had finished painting he faced the camera and sang Maclean's song *Vincent* with the portrait head acting as backdrop.

Van Gogh's symbolic imagery is extremely powerful in its emotional impact and impresses even those who are generally unmoved by art; this explains why one constantly finds reproductions of the Sunflower series or the Arles landscapes in the most unexpected settings. It is not possible to estimate accurately how many reproductions of Van Gogh's works have been produced – few statistics are available – but they must run into millions and Van Gogh can confidently be placed among the top ten most popular artists in terms of postcard sales: one hundred and eleven of his pictures are currently being reproduced. Vincent wanted his paintings to be appreciated by ordinary people and although the major exhibitions of his work are always well attended this has been achieved not so much by the originals as by surrogates of them, that is illustrations, reproductions and slides. (I should add that Vincent himself would not have disapproved of this.)

Apart from André Malraux, Walter Benjamin and John Berger, few writers on art have paid much attention to the phenomenon of reproductions and their influence on our perception of original works of art. Berger maintains that reproductions alter the unique status of the original artwork: it becomes merely the *"original of a reproduction"*, a kind of matrix or mould from which millions of copies are manufactured.[16] However, the photographic process does not create an exact equivalent of the original. Usually reproductions are reduced in scale; their colour and tonal values are different; their surface textures are totally unlike that of painted canvas. Copies are also made from copies and faithfulness to the original deteriorates alarmingly. It is commonly remarked that many people find original artworks crude in execution and dull in colour after a diet of glossy, garish reproductions.

Furthermore, as Berger points out, reproductions lend themselves to purposes completely alien to the function of the original, as when they are employed by advertising to add the status of art to consumer goods and services. Here are a few examples relating to Van Gogh: in Italy Vincent's paintings have been reproduced as decoration on sachets of sugar; in England they have been reproduced on cardboard plaques and offered to motorists as an incentive to buy a certain brand of petrol; the safe carriage of his canvases across the world has been used to advertise the reliability of a Scandinavian airline; portraits of Vincent and his brother Theo have been used by American and English advertising agencies to epitomise the combination of creative flair and business acumen that the agencies claim to possess;[17] publishers have promoted books on Van Gogh by issuing broadsheets covered by a splurge of violently coloured reproductions of his work, including details from the paintings wrenched out of context (with headlines such as *'Great art out of total despair'*); an American firm markets jigsaws of Van Gogh's landscapes; the tourist industry has also found Vincent's art and name useful: the French national tourist board have used his landscapes to advertise Provence; Vincent's name adorns hotels and restaurants in Europe; English holiday firms offer tours of *'Van Gogh country'* (Provence).

In his study of the industrialisation of culture, John McHale describes how symbolic images, particularly those drawn from the fine arts, are replicated by mass production techniques and then diffused on a world-wide scale, at ever-increasing speed, through the mass communication channels.[18] Thus images become expendable. (George Melly, in a review of Sharp's *Art book* suggests that reproduction, by making us over familiar with famous art works, devalues our perception of them and the appeal of Sharp's absurd juxtapositions is that they recharge the image for us, temporarily.)[19] McHale also points out that images undergo a cycle of transformations as they pass from one communication channel to another: *"transference through various modes changes both form and content – the new image can no longer be judged in the previous canon"*.[20]

Advertisers can even evoke the Van Gogh legend without using any reproductions of his paintings. This is possible because the basic information about him – a painter of Provence, sun-worship, sunflowers, etc – is known to millions. For example, an advertisement for Benson & Hedges special filter cigarettes (sold in a gold coloured pack) depicts, photographically, a field of sunflowers, a golden sunrise, an unfinished landscape painting on a portable easel (executed by James Winterbottom, an artist-teacher on the staff of a British art college) and, in the foreground, a palette, tubes of yellow pigment, brushes, and a straw hat. The image is completed by the caption *'Golden impressions'*. Thus by photographing a series of stage props in a natural setting the advertisers are able to harness the power of Van Goghism to sell a product.

What is significant about the mass replication and commercialisation of Van Gogh's art is that it destroys what Benjamin terms the 'aura' of artworks: their authenticity and uniqueness as originals, their historical specificity. To recuperate the particular meaning of a Van Gogh painting and for whom it was intended, the viewer now finds it necessary to isolate the man from the myth, to disentangle the primary objects from their husk of secondary imitations, and to reconstruct in imagination their historical and social context. Few consumers of the Van Gogh industry are willing to make this effort. Many art educators favour the popularisation of art. They argue that a person introduced to Van Gogh via a song, a popular biography, or a print will automatically absorb something of the original and that he or she will then graduate to a fuller appreciation of his work. But, for the reasons cited above, this seems unlikely to happen in the vast majority of cases.

It is clear than Van Gogh's labour during his lifetime has since yielded an immense amount of surplus value.[21] Vincent and Theo did not benefit from this surplus value but succeeding generations have done so, especially those who inherited Theo's collection of his brother's paintings and the Van Gogh archive, in particular Van Gogh's nephew, Dr. V. W. Van Gogh. Vincent's nephew has donated his collection to the Dutch state therefore it is the Dutch nation as a whole which has reaped a major portion of the surplus value of the Van Gogh estate. The Dutch are unlikely to realise the monetary value of Van Gogh's paintings (over £40 million) by selling them on the open market but the mere presence of the Van Gogh museum in Amsterdam serves as a draw for foreign tourists and its contents have substantially increased the number of artistic treasures owned by the Dutch nation. In other words, the accumulation of artworks in public museums is comparable to the accumulation of capital, though in this instance the reserve is not in the form of gold but art. When new artworks are added to the existing stock what increases is not merely the monetary wealth of a nation but the richness of its culture.

The democratisation of art and culture is not, however, an unmixed blessing as Marcuse pointed out in *One dimensional man* : *"the cultural centre is becoming a fitting part of the shopping centre, or municipal centre, or government centre. Domination has its own aesthetics, and democratic domination has its democratic aesthetics"*.[22] Artworks tend either to affirm or oppose the status quo. In Van Gogh's case his artistic project was undoubtedly antagonistic to the ethos of the bourgeois society and the Dutch by incorporating his works as part of the high culture of such a society contain their antagonistic force, reduce their sense of estrangement; in this way the contradiction between the artist's work and society is nullified.

The Van Gogh industry illustrates some of the most important moral dilemmas facing the contemporary artist. Vincent was a socially conscious artist: he was keen to found an artists' co-operative; he identified himself with the proletariat and depicted them in their hovels and at their toil; his ambition was to create an art that would console ordinary people. His work has reached many millions yet this has been accomplished at a price, in the ways already outlined. His art has been assimilated by the cultural establishment, its aesthetic appeal has been divorced from its social content, his life has been cannibalised by the mass media, his most excruciating personal humiliations have been made the butt of cartoonist's jokes. One wonders what Van Gogh's attitude to his work would have been if he could have predicted its fate; at least the contemporary artist knows the penalties of 'success'.

The art of painting is a pre-capitalist mode of production which has continued into the capitalist era. As a painter Van Gogh inherited a long tradition of hand craftsmanship and he produced unique artifacts. These characteristics of painting are at variance with machine production, and the mass replication of imagery typical of industrialised society. Yet we have seen how easily his work has been absorbed and turned into a commodity by that society. In recent years a significant number of contemporary artists in Europe and the United States have developed a new social awareness and are seeking to produce artworks which will resist assimilation and which are designed to overcome the political impotency of art. However, the continued buoyancy of the Van Gogh industry demonstrates how intractable are the problems involved in such an enterprise. A. M. Hammacher remarks: *"As a symbol Van Gogh lives in a society which is still at odds with art, so that his symbol does not, unfortunately, mean that art has now found roots in the people"*.[23]

(55) *Images from the van Gogh industry (2)*

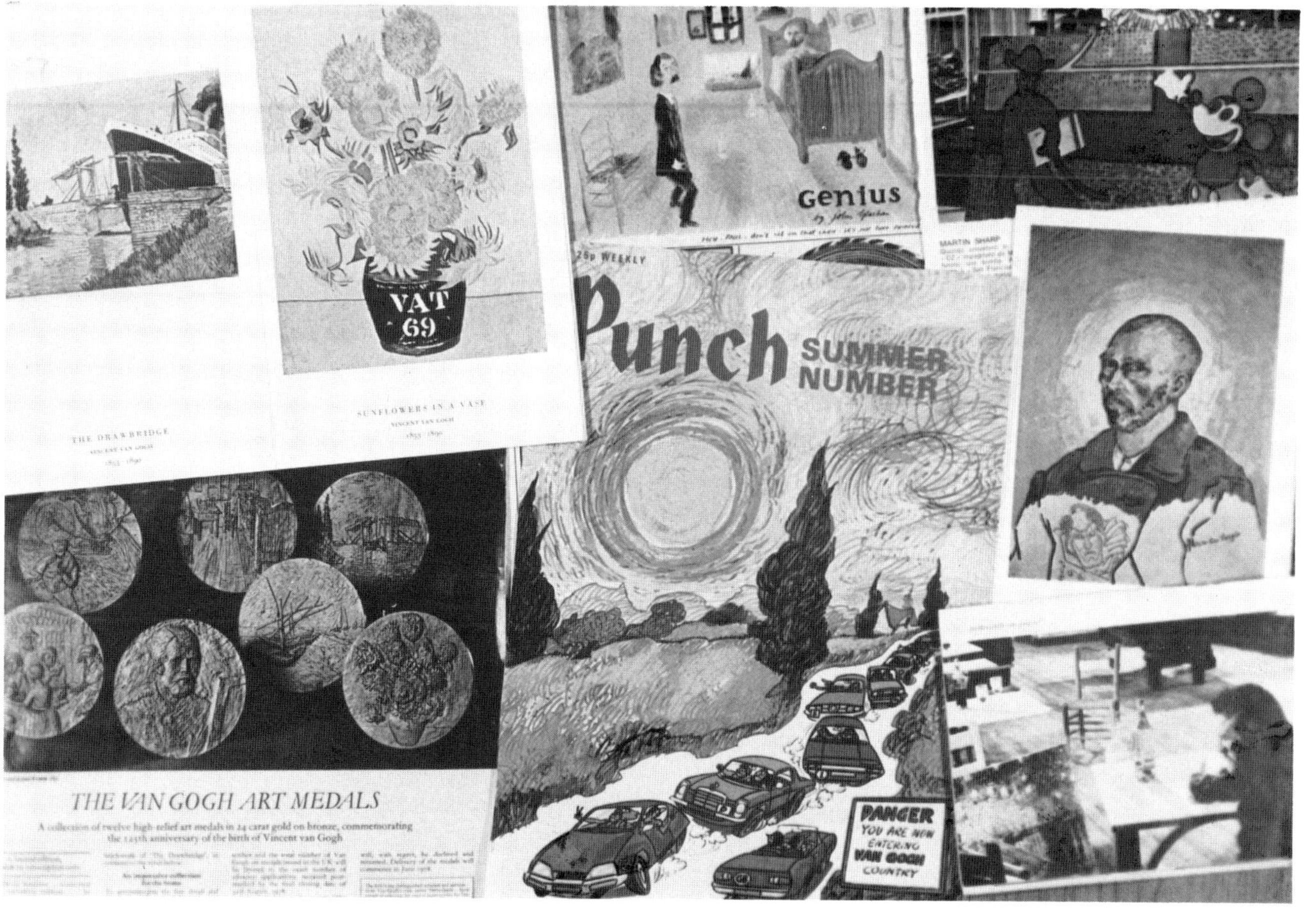

Notes and references:

1. Jean Cassou 'Art and confrontation' – essay in-*Art and confrontation: France and the arts in an age of change* (Studio Vista, 1970) p 14.

2. A. M. Hammacher, in a detailed review of the literature on Van Gogh to date, claims that 1935 – the year in which the first edition of *Lust for Life* was published – marked the beginning of the great popular cult of Van Gogh. Hammacher recognises the existence of the Van Gogh industry and claims that it is a social phenomenon compounded of *"a blend of sensation . . . ethics of suffering . . . powerful colour".* He also notes a post-1945 boom in this industry and describes how *"a kind of Van Gogh semiology developed, a socio-aesthetic Van Gogh language, people beginning to live according to Van Gogh symbols".*
A. M. Hammacher 'Van Gogh and the words' – in-*The works of Vincent Van Gogh his paintings and drawings* by J-B de la Faille(Weidenfeld and Nicolson, 1970) pp 9–37. Michael Gough, an actor who played the part of Van Gogh in a BBC television documentary described in Radio Times (October 12, 1972 pp 8–9) how he simulated the life of Van Gogh for five months. Gough himself did not speak to anyone for days at a time, he lived on coffee and brandy and worked in the boiling heat, in imitation of Van Gogh's habits.

3. *Auction* 3 (8) April 1970.

4. J-B de la Faille. *The works of Vincent Van Gogh:his paintings and drawings* (Weidenfeld and Nicolson, 1970).

5. Derrick Greaves 'Homage to Van Gogh' *Art and Artists* December 1968 pp 24–25.

6. John Russell *Francis Bacon* (Thames and Hudson, 1971) p 92.

7. Christopher Finch 'Clive Barker' *Art and Artists* January 1968 pp 16–19.

8. Adrian Henri *Environments and Happenings* (Thames and Hudson, 1974) p 70 (illus p 55).

9. Martin Sharp *Artbook* (Mathews Miller Dunbar, 1972). *Oz* magazine featured several of Sharp's Van Gogh artoons but this did not indicate that the Underground/Counter-culture/Psychedelic sensibility was receptive to art generally, it was only interested in 'mad' artists such as Van Gogh and Richard Dadd because they conformed to the norms of extreme subjectivity, freakiness and genius required by Underground culture. Consequently *Oz* never featured Cézanne, Mondrian or the Cubist works of Picasso.

10. Ward Kimball *Art afterpieces* (New York, Essandess Special Edition, Simon & Schuster, 1964).

11. I am indebted to Peter Webb for this information and the loan of material on Van Gogh.

12. Stuart Hall & Paddy Whannel *The popular arts* (Hutchinson, 1964) p 423.

13. John Berger 'The difficulty of being an artist' – in– *Permanent red: essays in seeing* (Methuen, 1960) pp 34–38.

14. *Arts in society* Winter 1960 pp 4–5.

15. Op cit (13).

16. John Berger *Ways of seeing* (BBC/Penguin Books, 1972) p 21.

17. *Campaign* April 28, 1972. p 2.

18. John McHale 'The plastic parthenon' – in – *Kitsch: an anthology of bad taste* ; ed. by Gillo Dorfles (Studio Vista, 1969) pp 98–110.

19. *The Guardian* December 28, 1972 p 12.

20. Op cit (18).

21. In reference to the manner in which artworks acquire value see the inconclusive discussion of this question in the April, May, July, August and September 1975 issues of *Art and Artists* . Not all artworks are highly valued by later generations hence it is necessary to account for the increase in surplus value in certain instances but not others. One reason which can be cited is that closely similar acts of labour performed by two different individuals yield two different values. This is simply the notion of skill: the act of drawing by a skilled hand yields a greater value than that by an unskilled hand. Marx explained that skill in the hand is stored-up labour power (it is the result of hours of practice). Also to be taken into consideration is the labour invested in Van Gogh's work by critics, dealers, collectors, curators, scholars, publishers, etc since the death of Van Gogh. This later point was made by Toni del Renzio in the July 1975 issue of *Art and Artists*.

22. Herbert Marcuse *One dimensional man* (Sphere Books, 1968) p 63.

23. Op cit (2).

VAN GOGH AS A PEASANT PAINTER

It would be erroneous to assert that van Gogh was exclusively a peasant painter because he depicted other subjects – flower pieces, self-portraits, landscapes, townscapes – besides peasants; nevertheless, images of peasants make up a large proportion of his artistic output and at various times during the early part of his artistic career he drew and painted little else.

Class origins

There is no uncertainty about Vincent's class origins. He was born into the Dutch petty bourgeoisie (his father was a parson, his uncles were art and print dealers, his cousin Anton Mauve was an artist). Because Vincent spent his youth in small villages where his father had been posted by the Church,he grew up in environments where the majority of those surrounding him were peasants. His companions at school were, therefore, peasant boys. In fact his parents withdrew him from the public primary school because they discovered that contact with the peasant boys was making him 'too rough'. Nevertheless, it was with miners and the poor peasantry that Vincent eventually identified emotionally rather than with the class into which he had been born. Indeed, there came a time when Vincent found the hypocrisy, self-righteousness, prudishness, and materialism of the Dutch middle class intolerable. In an early letter to Theo Vincent declared:*"Being a labourer, I feel at home in the labouring class, and more and more I will try to live and take root there"*.[1]

Character and political attitudes

Vincent came from a deeply religious, puritanical background in which the idea of service to humanity was paramount. Most of his life Vincent was lonely; he never married or had a fully satisfactory relationship with a woman even though he longed to found a family of his own. To fulfil his sexual needs Vincent had to resort to prostitutes. He is often thought of as a primitive individual but in fact he was extremely literate, he was widely travelled, and he was fluent in three languages. He detested useless study, nevertheless he was an intellectual. Despite his sympathy for the poor and oppressed, his class origin, his learning, his temperament, and his vocation as an artist, kept him isolated from the people he wished to serve. He did not take part in their collective struggles directly; he did not, for example, join a trade union or a political party or depict the positive aspects of the workers' struggle hence his pictures of them tend to be gloomy, melancholy and despairing even when the colours he uses are at their brightest.

The family situation into which he was born encouraged in him a morbid fascination with death and for psychological reasons he was receptive to the ethic of suffering propagated by Christianity (the idea of redemption through suffering).

In consequence it was easy for Vincent to find in the objective world examples of suffering that corresponded to his subjective feelings of misery. What was internal found external justification, what was private and individual became public and social.

Julius Meier-Graefe, in an early study of Vincent (1906), declared unequivocally that van Gogh was a Socialist but his article did not provide any hard evidence for this claim.[2] There is, however, at least one letter to Theo which reveals Vincent's political convictions. In this letter Vincent discusses certain political events in France and Delacroix's explicitly political painting *'Liberty leading the people'* and then declares that in any revolution he would expect Theo to side with the government forces and himself with the insurrectionists. He continues: *"Neither you nor I meddle with politics, but we live in a the world, in society, and involuntarily ranks of people group themselves . . . As an individual, one is part of all humanity. This humanity is divided into parties. How much is it one's own free will, how much is it the fatality of circumstances which makes one belong to one party or to its opposite?"*.[3] It is clear from this letter that van Gogh was fully aware of the divisions of wealth and class characteristic of European society and that his sympathy was with the forces of change and revolution. Indeed, his ideas are almost Marxist when he acknowledges that an individual's class position is determined by social factors independent of that person's will.

Popular imagery

Vincent, like Courbet before him, was intensely interested in popular imagery. One type of popular imagery that he collected assiduously and studied avidly were the wood engravings that appeared in English illustrated magazines such as the *Graphic* and the *Illustrated London News*.[4] One series run by the *Graphic* appealed to him especially, that is, a series entitled *'Heads of the people'*, a series which depicted workers from different trades, for

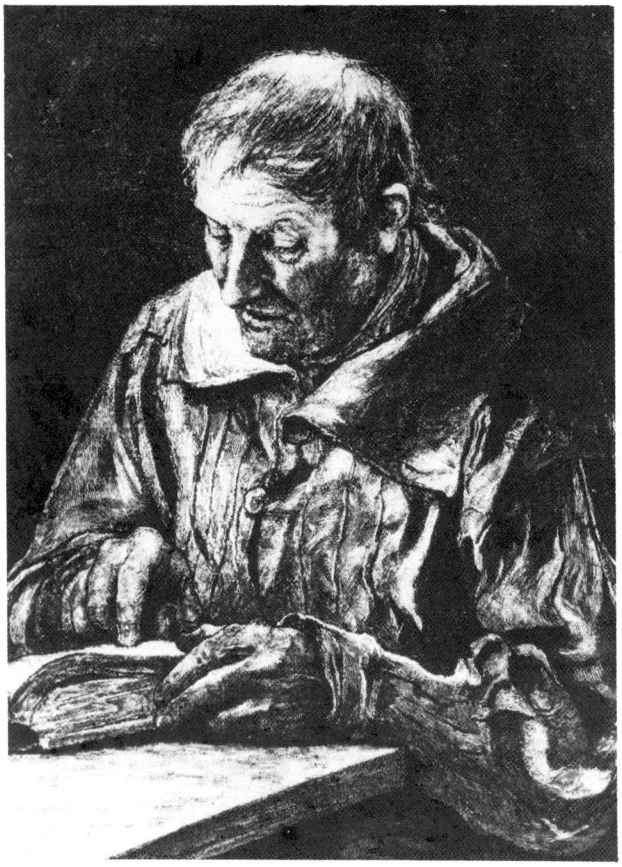

(56) **H. Herkomer,** *Heads of the people 2: the agricultural labourer, Sunday.* **The Graphic 9 October 1875, wood-engraving.**

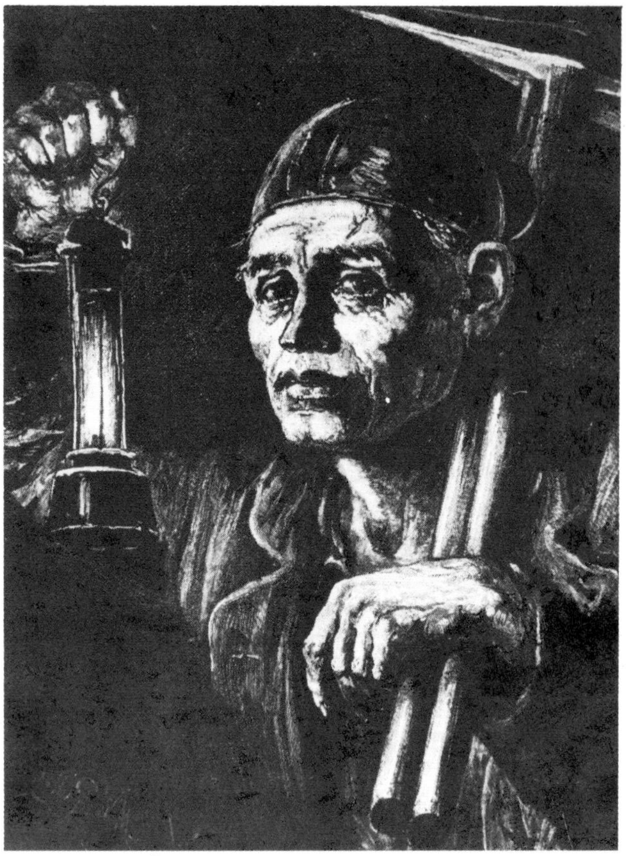

(57) **M. W. Ridley,** *Heads of the people 6: the miner* **The Graphic 15 April 1876, wood-engraving.**

example, mining, agriculture, coastguarding, etc. Vincent emulated this series in his own art by producing a number of paintings entitled *'Heads of peasants'* and by producing portraits of a peasant and a postman in Arles. (Bruegel's head of a peasant seen in profile can also be cited as an historical precedent for these portraits.) Within English painting and illustration during the 1860s and 1870s there was a strong vein of social realism – images of workers, pictures of homelessness, the workhouses, opium dens, soup kitchens, unemployment, industrial accidents, prisons, etc – prompted by the vile conditions of the mass of the population under early capitalism. Such images moved Vincent profoundly; he regarded them as serious, noble and true. Above all it was their sentiment and warmth that appealed to him. They seemed to him to embody expressions of sympathy on the part of the artists towards those depicted. French caricaturists, such as Gavarni and Daumier, also treated similar subjects but, as Vincent explained in a letter to Rappard in 1882, he preferred the English illustrators because they did not, like Gavarni and Daumier, *"look on society with malice"*.[5] This 'malice' was the result of the more highly developed class and political consciousness of the French satirists; it was also a sign that the class struggle in France had been more intense and bitter than in Britain or Holland. It is clear that at this point in time Vincent's understanding of politics was somewhat limited.

Prints for the people

While at The Hague in November 1882 Vincent had a series of drawings turned into lithographs. A workman asked if he could hang one of these prints on the wall of his workplace. Vincent was delighted: *"No result of my work could please me better than that ordinary working people would hang such prints in their room or workshop"*[6] For a while Vincent toyed with the idea of becoming a professional illustrator, (in which case his art might have reached a wide public in his own lifetime) but one reason why he did not pursue the idea was that he disliked working to order.

However, his letters to Theo during the autumn and winter months of 1882 reveal an obsession with the idea of democratising art production, in particular *"making figures* ***from the people for the people***". He advocates that *"Dutch drawings be made, printed, and distributed which are destined for workmen's houses and for farms, in a word for every working man..."* He envisaged *"a combination of artists"* working not for commercial gain but *"as a matter of public service and duty"* and distributing prints *"in a popular edition"*. Unfortunately Vincent's scheme came to nothing. The idea of an artists' co-operative or collective remained with him for the rest of his life. His attempt to found 'a studio in the South' with

Gauguin in the Yellow House at Arles in 1888 was another effort in this direction. Such schemes reflected the dissatisfaction which many artists felt with the extreme individualism of artistic practice in the nineteenth century.

Patronage

As is well known, Vincent sold virtually nothing during his lifetime. Despite his emotional identification with the working class and his schemes for democratising art production Vincent's work as a painter was bound to be directed towards the urban bourgeoisie because it was the only section of the public which could afford art and had the leisure and education to attend art exhibitions. Vincent's drawings and paintings were dispatched to Paris, to his brother Theo who was by profession a dealer in art. Theo acted, in effect, as Vincent's patron, his only patron. And since Theo supported Vincent by means of a regular salary his role was that of a capitalist employer, one who gains possession of the output of his wage-labourers to sell at a profit. Of course, Vincent hoped that his depictions of peasants would benefit them ultimately: one purpose of his painting was to arouse the social consciences of the wealthy to the plight of the poor. Eventually Vincent's work did become truly popular – as a result of state patronage, public exhibitions, the writings of various art critics, and the mass replication of images made possible by photographic reproduction – but by then Vincent and the peasants in his pictures were dead.

The most astonishing enigma of Vincent's oeuvre is the lack of single portrait of his brother Theo to whom he owed so much.

Vincent's peasant paintings

Since Vincent had worked as a young man in art and print shops and visited numerous art exhibitions in three European capitals, he was extremely knowledgable about the art of the past and of his own day. Vincent admired the work of many artists but it was perhaps Millet's that impressed him most, especially when he himself decided to paint the life of the Dutch peasantry. In 1885 he told Theo: *"I have no other wish than to live deep, deep in the heart of the countryside and paint the life of the peasants. I feel that I can create for myself a sphere of work, and so I intend to keep my hand on the plough and cut my furrow".*[7] Note the agricultural metaphor in the last sentence. Vincent had read Sensier's biography of Millet in which the observation is made that Millet's peasants look as if they were painted with the earth they till. In his writings and art practice

(58) *Peasant woman, head,* Nuenen 1885, oil on canvas, 37.5 x 28 cm, Otterlo, Rijksmuseum Kröller-Müller.

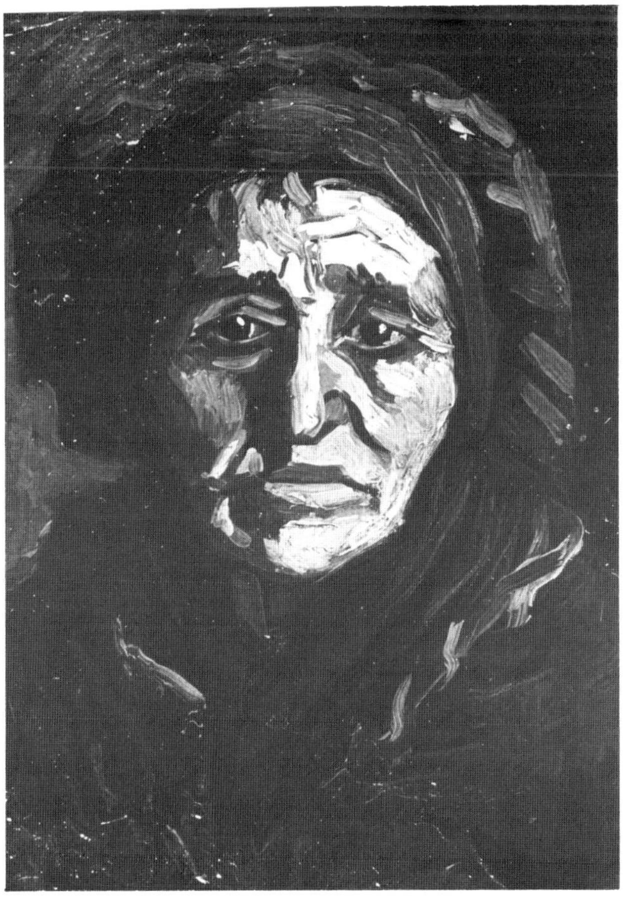

(59) *Old man with his head in his hands ('At eternity's gate'),* The Hague 1882, lithograph, 55.5 x 36.5 cm, Various collections.

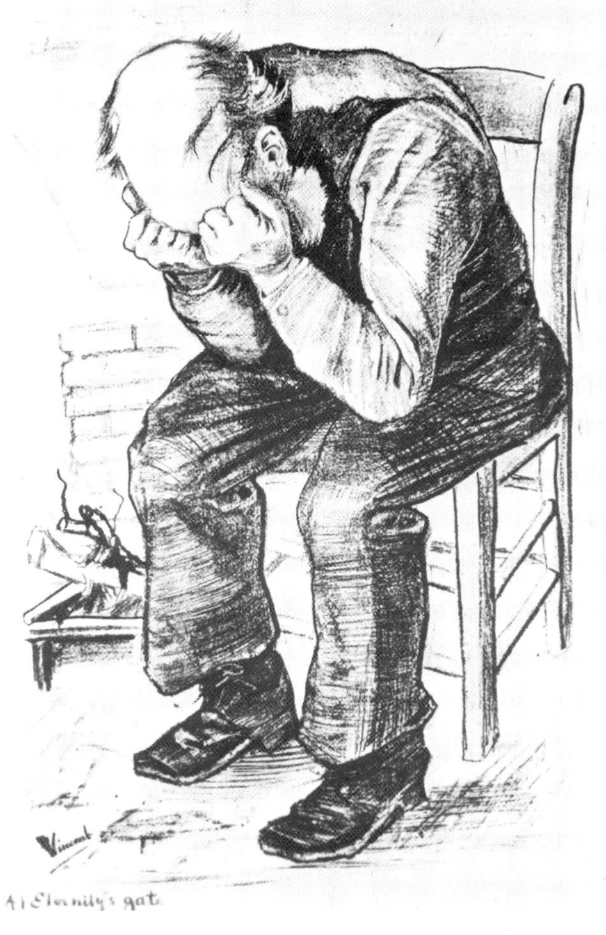

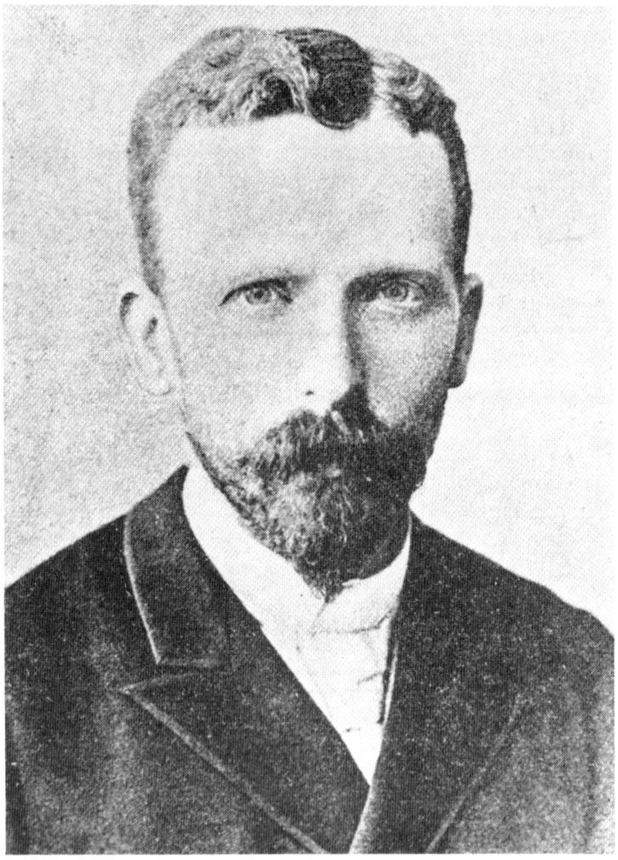

(**60**) *Theo van Gogh.*

Vincent makes a metaphorical equation between his work as a painter and that of the peasantry: the blank canvas becomes a field; the material of pigment and certain of its tones and hues become earth; the brush becomes a plough; the brush-strokes become furrows; the act of creation becomes sowing. The metaphor also has a quasi-religious undertone: the painter, like God, is a creator; God used clay to mould mankind; the artist moulds images of human beings from earth-coloured pigments.

A similar correspondence between style and subject matter, means and ends, is to be found in Vincent's drawings. In a perceptive essay on a drawing by van Gogh, Fritz Novotny explains the *"system of angular volumes"* which Vincent developed during his Dutch period in these terms: *"This form is part of the 'rustic' style that van Gogh used to express his idea of the peasant"*.[8]

Work

It is difficult for us now, familiar as we are with the non-naturalistic images of twentieth century avant garde art, to recapture the initial impact of Vincent's paintings on his contemporaries. We can only gain some inkling of their shock-value by comparing them to the French Salon paintings and the British Royal Academy paintings dating from the same period. In general, these latter pictures are neat and tidy, harmoniously composed, smoothly surfaced, minutely detailed, highly finished and sentimental. Vincent's peasant paintings, on the other hand, are vigorous, broad in conception, crudely composed, roughly textured, sketch-like, and unsentimental. What they reveal is firstly, Vincent's profound understanding of the physical work done by peasants (the subject of work occupies a central place in the paintings of the Dutch period; Vincent's aim was not to present a general statement about work by showing different kinds of labour within the same canvas, as in Ford Maddox Brown's famous, overcrowded picture *'Work'* (1852–65), but to document the specific work tasks of peasants and weavers); and secondly, the work of the artist (that is, by using thick paint in which the trace of the brush is clearly visible Vincent foregrounded rather than disguised the artistic labour required to generate his pictures). The peasant's struggle with the earth was analogous to Vincent's struggle with paint; Vincent sought to communicate the first by means of the second. Van Gogh's paintings exemplify work and for this reason they are exemplary – in the sense that they show how a sense of sympathy and solidarity can exist between the artist–intellectuals of the world and the manual workers of the world. In many respects the two groups are divided but in work they are united. Van Gogh worked as hard and as long as the peasants in the fields. His artistic labour was equivalent to, and represented in the sphere of art, their labour in the sphere of agriculture. In short, van Gogh's Dutch

(61) *Peasant woman digging,* Nuenen 1885, oil on canvas on panel, 42.3 x 32.3 cm, Birmingham, Barber Institute of Fine Art, University of Birmingham.

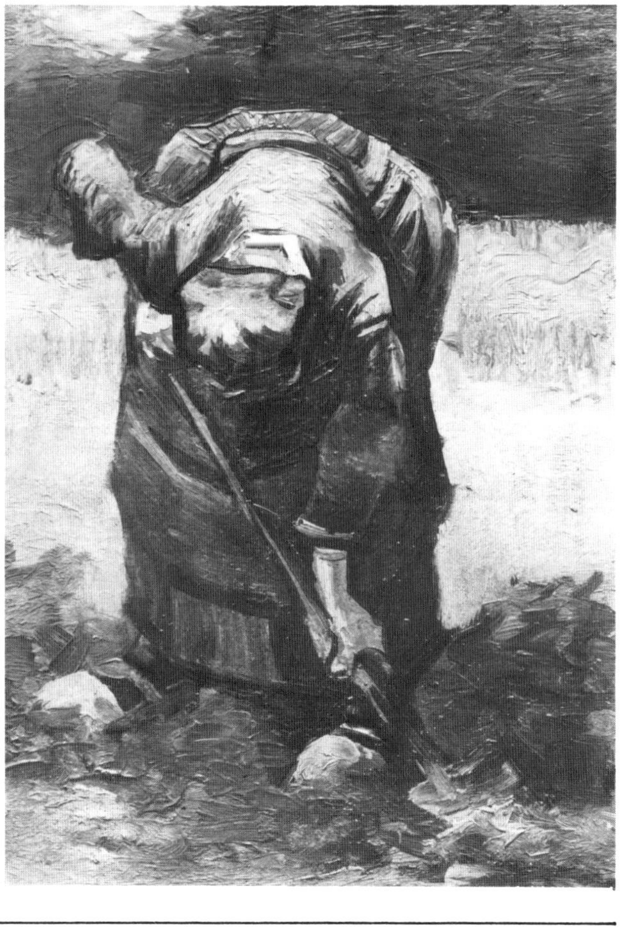

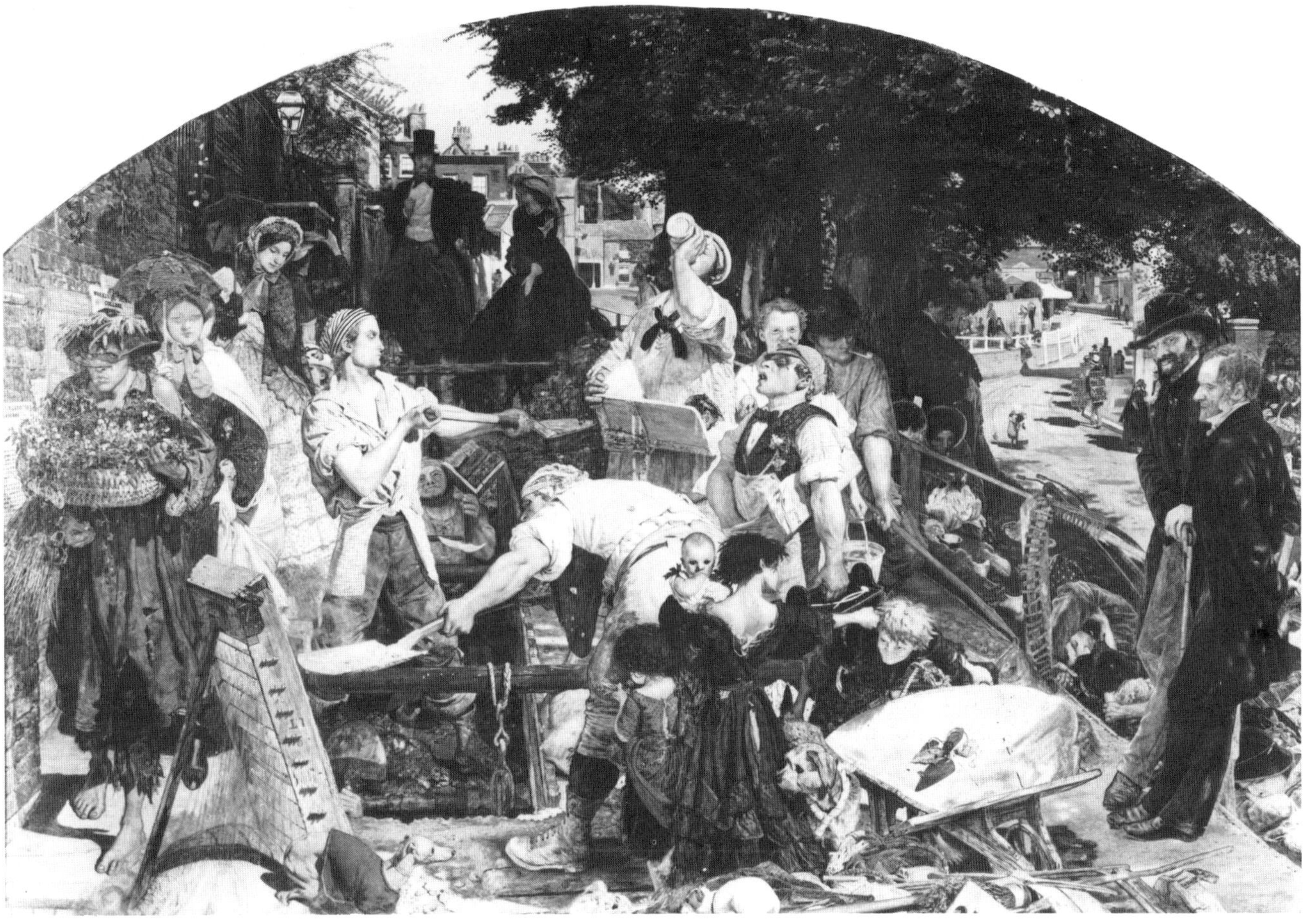

(62) Ford Maddox-Brown, *Work,* 1852-65, oil on canvas, Manchester, City Art Gallery.

(63) *Peasant with sickle,* Nuenen 1885, black chalk, 43.5 x 55.5, Amsterdam, Rijksmuseum Vincent van Gogh.

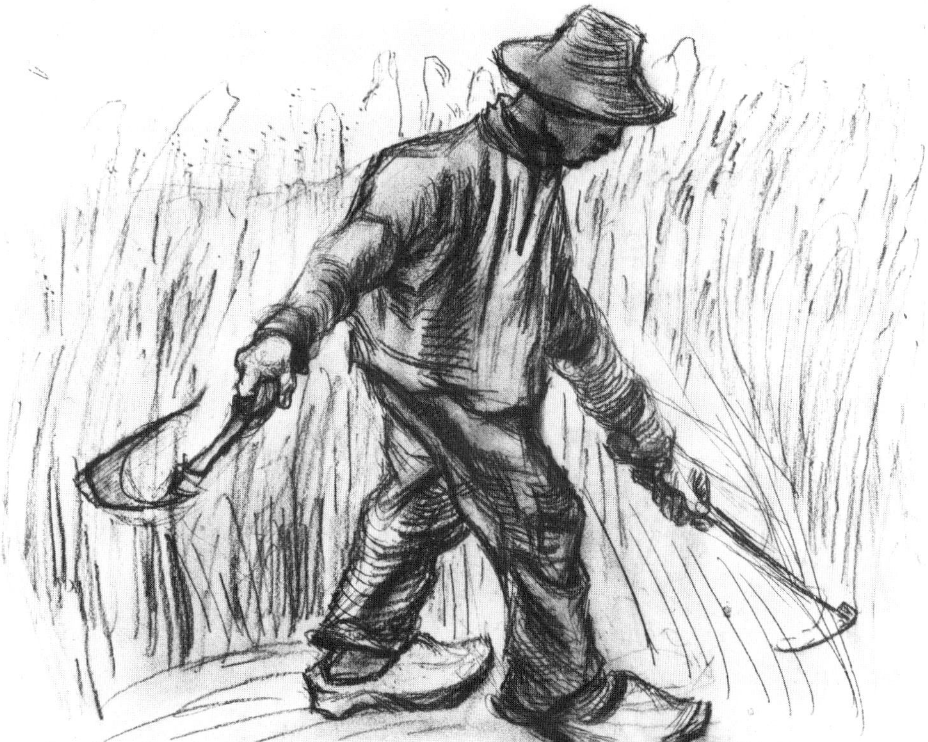

paintings were an extended homage to manual labour – they celebrated, dignified and memoralized it.

During his Dutch period van Gogh produced hundreds of drawings and paintings of peasant life. The sheer quantity of works which have survived indicate that van Gogh's objective was an intensive and systematic documentation of the character, labour, family life and habitat of the Dutch peasantry. His project can be compared to those undertaken by nineteenth century anthropologists in relation to non-European primitive and tribal communities. To depict the daily work tasks of the peasants Vincent followed them into the fields and into their homes. He made detailed studies of their hands, their clothing and their sparsely furnished straw-thatched mud huts (these huts reminded him of the nests which birds construct for their comfort). At the same time he copied reproductions of Millet's images of peasants in order to improve his draughtsmanship and his knowledge of typical poses.

There are no bird's eye viewpoints in Vincent's depictions of peasants. We, the spectators, are placed at their level – ground level. Vincent moves in close to give us an intimate picture of their daily lives. Judging from the evidence of his paintings and drawings the peasants he studied were poor peasants working small, unprofitable plots of land. We learn from his studies that women did as much if not more of the back-breaking toil in the fields. The peasants needed to subsidize their living from the land in other ways, as the pictures of women spinning in order to provide clothing for their families, or as a source of extra income, indicate. The poor depressed peasants of Holland were thus very different from the proud peasant proprietors of France such as we find celebrated in Courbet's *'Peasants from Flagey returning from the fair'.*

Sometimes van Gogh had difficulty gaining the confidence of the peasants who tended to regard him as an eccentric and who refused to pose for him. On the other hand, many peasants welcomed the small sums of money which he paid in return for posing. In some instances van Gogh painted the same individual or peasant family over and over again (for example, the members of the De Groot family who provided the figures for the *'Potato eaters'*). Since these studies were frequently executed in the homes of the peasants it is reasonable to assume that Vincent developed a friendly relationship with a number of his sitters. One report claims that a local priest tried to prevent the peasants from posing for Vincent on the grounds that the painter was a bad moral influence. (Vincent has sketched a pregnant female peasant and it was suspected, wrongly, that he was responsible for the girl's condition.)

As already mentioned,Vincent was fascinated by death and by graveyards. At Nuenen he made several studies of a ruined church tower and a peasant cemetery. His remarks relating to these studies indicate how fatalism and the cyclical concept of time informed Vincent's view of the peasantry: *"I wanted to express how these ruins show that* **for ages** *the peasants had been laid to rest in the very fields which they dug up when alive – I wanted to express what a simple thing death and burial is, just as simple as the falling of an autumn leaf – just a bit of earth dug up – a wooden cross. The fields around, where the grass of the churchyard ends, beyond the little wall, form a last line against the horizon – like the horizon of the sea".* Since the church tower was to be demolished Vincent recognised that religion is subject to historical change but even so it did not alter his view of the peasantry: *"And now those ruins tell me how a faith and a religion moldered away – strongly founded though they were – but how the life and death of the peasants remain forever the same, budding and withering regularly, like the grass and the flowers growing there in that churchyard".* [9]

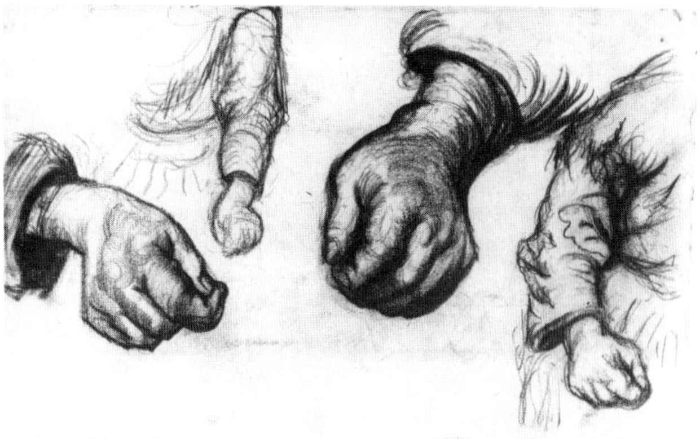

(64) *Two hands and two arms,* Nuenen 1885, black chalk, 20 x 33 cm, Amsterdam, Rijksmuseum Vincent van Gogh.

The four seasons project

In the summer of 1884 Vincent met, in Eindhoven, a sixty year old man called Hermans. Hermans was wealthy – he had been a goldsmith –

(65) *Peasant cemetary,* Nuenen 1885, oil on canvas, 63 x 79 cm, Amsterdam, Rijksmuseum Vincent van Gogh.

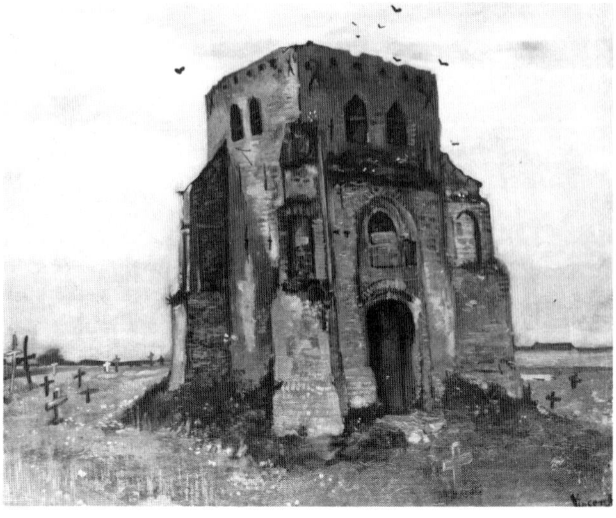

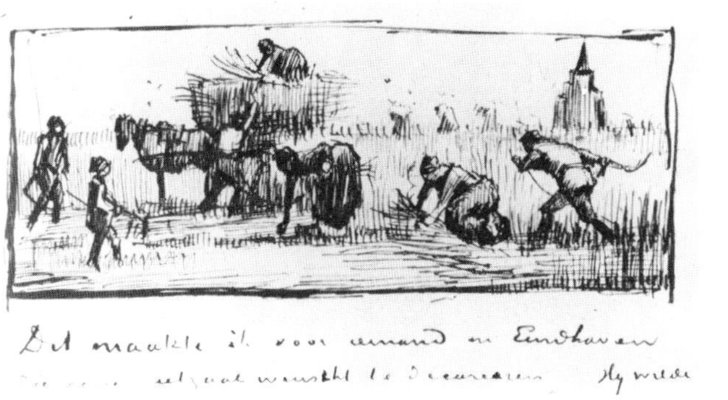

(66) *Wheatharvest,* Nuenen 1884, pen and ink sketch in letter 374 to Theo, Amsterdam, Rijksmuseum Vincent van Gogh.

and had a house full of antiques. He was also an amateur painter; Vincent helped him to improve his technique. Hermans was decorating his house himself and wanted a series of paintings of saints to embellish his dining room. Vincent persuaded him that images of local peasant life also symbolizing the seasons would be more appropriate motifs. (The tradition of images of peasant life representing the seasons produced for wealthy businessmen dates back to Bruegel and beyond.) Since Hermans wanted to paint the panels himself, Vincent provided him with designs on a reduced scale.

At that time Vincent was much concerned with problems of colour theory. Each season, he reflected, could be represented by a colour scheme dominated by a pair of complementary colours, that is, spring could be represented by red and green, summer by blue and orange, autumn by yellow and violet, and winter by black and white. These colours were not chosen arbitrarily; they had a basis in empirical observation, for example, the red and green combination for spring derived from the pink of apple blossom and the green of young corn. These colours were linked in Vincent's mind to a particular emotion; in the case of spring, for example, it was 'tenderness'. The sketches and studies for the series do not do justice to the originality of Vincent's thought; however, amongst the landscapes of the Arles period there are pictures in which the idea of representing the mood of a season primarily through a contrast of colours is fulfilled.

Potato studies

While at Nuenen Vincent painted a series of studies of piles of potatoes. Flowers, fruit and vegetables were, of course, favourite subjects of the Dutch masters of the past, therefore Vincent's potato studies must be seen as a continuation of this genre. However, one has only to compare his studies to the opulent still-life paintings of the Dutch tradition to realise how polemical Vincent's choice of subject matter was: he deliberately chose the most mundane, the most humble, the most unpicturesque food available. As we know from Vincent's major work of the Dutch period *'The potato eaters'*, potatoes were the staple diet of the poor peasants of that time. The peasants grew

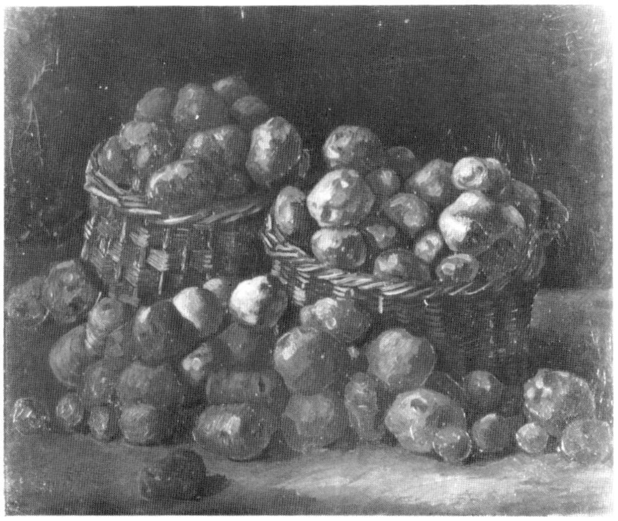

(67) *Still life with two baskets of potatoes,* Nuenen 1885, oil on canvas, 66 x 79 cm, Amsterdam, Rijksmuseum Vincent van Gogh.

potatoes, they ate potatoes, they were covered by earth like potatoes, they were humble like potatoes, and in their dark, grubby clothes huddled together in their huts they even looked like potatoes; they *were* potatoes. Vincent was not the only person to use potatoes as a metaphor for peasants: in 1850 Karl Marx claimed that the great mass of the French nation consisted of peasant small holdings added together *"much as potatoes in a sack form a sack of potatoes".*[10]

'The potato eaters'

There are several detailed studies of Vincent's *'The potato eaters'* (1885), the masterpiece of his Dutch period, therefore I will merely quote his own remarks which spell out the picture's moralizing and didactic function, and which justify its coarseness of execution on the grounds of appropriateness to its theme: *"I have tried to emphasize that those people, eating their potatoes in the lamplight, have dug the earth with those very hands they put in the dish, and so it speaks of* ***manual labour****, and how they have honestly earned their food.*

I wanted to give the impression of a way of life quite different from that of us civilized people. Therefore I am not at all anxious for everyone to like it or to admire it at once.

All winter long I have had the threads of this tissue in my hands, and have searched for the ultimate pattern; and though it has become a tissue of rough coarse aspect, nevertheless the threads have been chosen carefully and according to certain rules. And it might prove to be a real ***peasant picture. I know it is****. . ."*

". . . it would be wrong, I think, to give a peasant picture a certain conventional smoothness. If a peasant picture smells of bacon, smoke, potato steam – all right, that's not unhealthy; if a stable smells of dung – all right, that belongs to a stable; if the field has an odour of ripe corn or potatoes or of guano or manure – that's healthy especially for

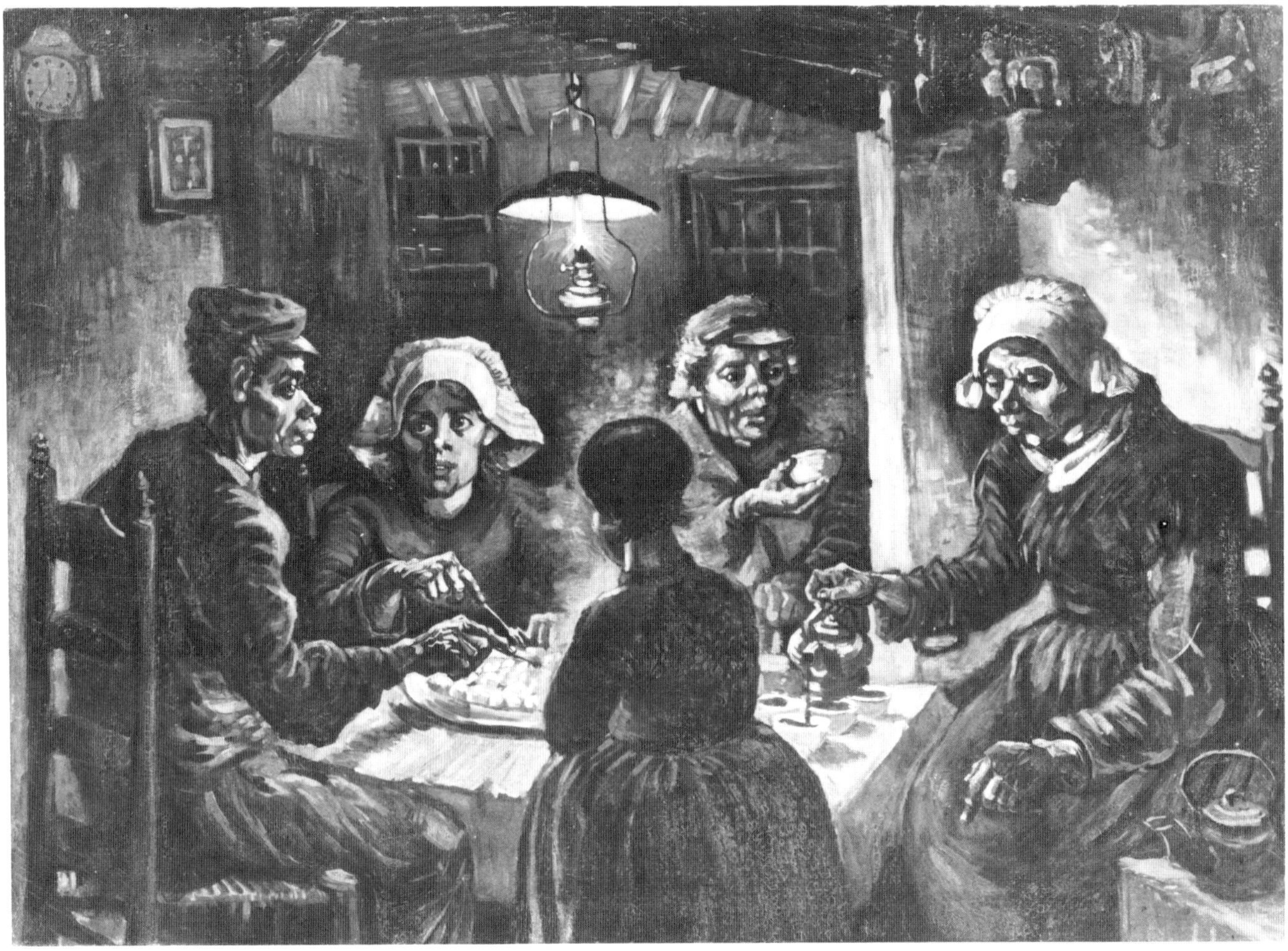

(68) *Potatoe eaters,* Nuenen 1885, oil on canvas, 82 x 114 cm, Amsterdam, Rijksmuseum Vincent van Gogh.

(69) Josef Israels,' The frugal meal', (1860-75?) 88.9 x 138.7 cm, oil on canvas, Glasgow Art Gallery, (first exhibited at the Paris Salon of 1876).

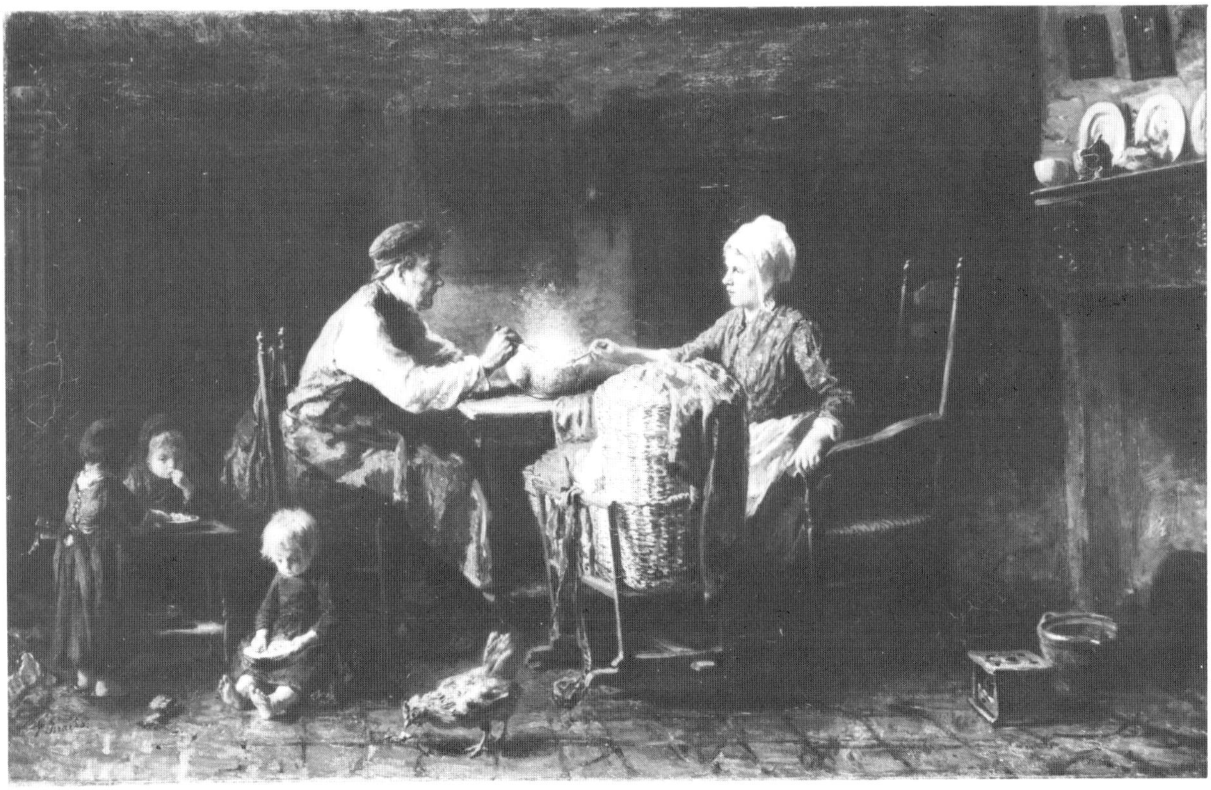

city people.

Such pictures may **teach** *them something. But to be perfumed is not what a peasant picture needs".*[11]

Even though its individual figures are somewhat self-absorbed, *'The potato eaters'* presents a powerful image of the family as a social institution. An image of the family engaged in an important unifying ritual, namely, the evening meal which ensures the reproduction of the family in both a physical and a social sense. Vincent consciously refused to record the domestic life of the Dutch middle classes, consequently there are no paintings of the van Gogh family at table. It was in the dim huts of the peasants that van Gogh seemed to find the warmth of family life which he missed in the house of his parents.

Weavers and coal miners

Besides peasants there were living at Nuenen some small craftsmen – weavers – whom Vincent recorded in murky huts framed by their looms. As Carl Nordenfalk explains, Vincent's *"interest was directed not only to the looms and their complicated construction, but also to the social realities behind them. The competition of modern manufacturing concerns was driving the old home industry out of existence, and the weavers of Nuenen had to slave for days on end to earn a subsistence. In some most expressive pictures van Gogh presents the weaver as a victim held fast in the spiked jaws of the loom, or as a captive in a medieval instrument of torture. The social significance is quite unmistakable".*[12] **Against this one can cite the fact that the weavers worked as part of a family in their own homes whereas once the factory system became dominant the family ceased to work as a unit.**

Although Vincent concentrated his attention upon the work of peasants and small craftsmen,he had first-hand knowledge of industrial labour, in particular coal mining. Previously, in the late 1870s, he had worked as a lay preacher amongst the small mining communities of the Borinage, a grim region of Southern Belgium. There he had personally witnessed the conditions miners faced underground and the appalling results of fire damp explosions in the pits. Vincent's descriptions of the miserable lives lived by the mining families are very moving and are now important social documents.

At Wasmes in the spring of 1879 Vincent spent six hours below ground with the miners, both men and women, in the Marcasse *"one of the oldest and most dangerous mines in the neighbourhood". "Most of the miners",* **Vincent explained to Theo,** *"are thin and pale from fever; they look tired and emaciated, weather-beaten and aged before their time. On the whole the women are faded and worn".*[13] **Young children of both sexes were also employed in the mine loading coal onto carts; Vincent claimed they never saw the light of day. There are several reports of Vincent's devoted medical help to injured and burnt miners following a fire damp explosion in the Agrappe pit. There**

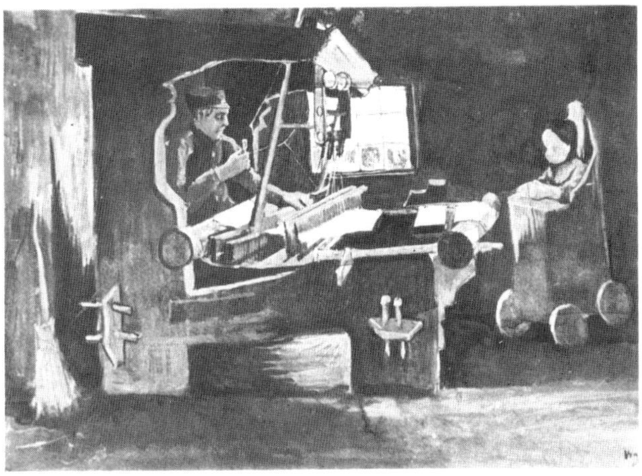

(70) *Weaver facing right,* **Nuenen 1884, watercolour, 30.5 x 43 cm, Location unknown.**

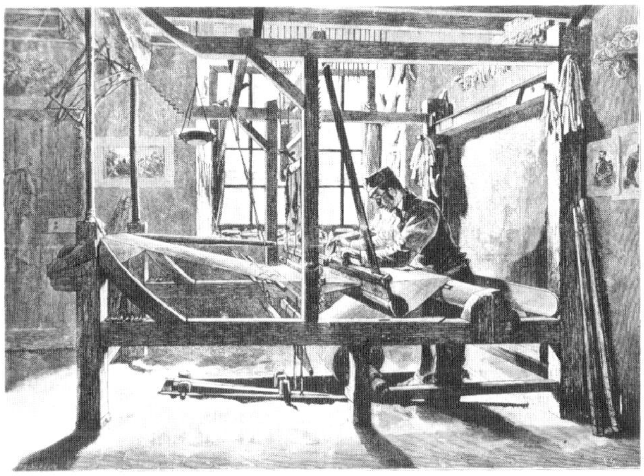

(71) Ryckebusch, *Les industries qui disparaissant – un tisserand,***wood-engraving by P. Grenier, L'Illustration 10 September 1881;collected by Vincent in 1884.**

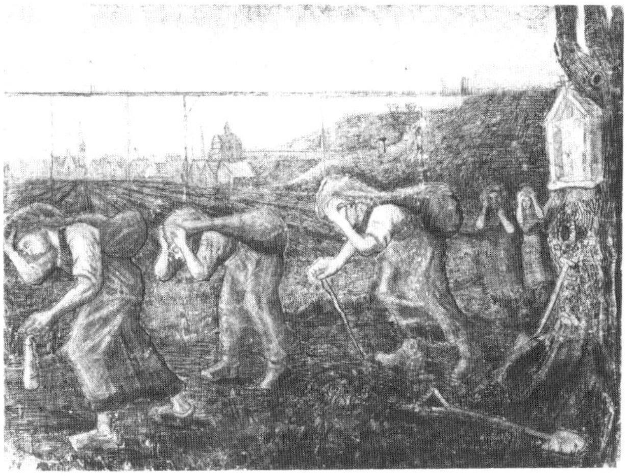

(72) *Miners' wives carrying coal sacks ('The bearers of the burden'),* **Brussels 1881, pen and pencil, washed, 43 x 60 cm, Otterlo, Rijksmuseum Kröller-Müller.**

is also another, uncorroborated report, that Vincent, shocked by the starvation earnings of the

miners, visited the mine owners and demanded that they increase the wage rates (he had no success). Legend also has it that during a strike Vincent was the only person from outside the mining community whose views the miners respected and that therefore they heeded his advice to desist from violence in pursuit of their demands. (Actually this report probably applies to a retired foreman described in one of Vincent's letters.)[14]

It was in the Borinage, following his failure to reconcile the example of Christ with the doctrines of the Church, that Vincent decided to make art his religion. Two of his earliest drawings are, therefore, of miner's wives carrying sacks of coal and of miners trudging to the shaft through the winter snow.

Provence

During the climax of his artistic career at Arles and St Rémy, Vincent's interest in the peasantry slackened somewhat: landscapes, still-lives, and portraits of town dwellers predominated. Even so, Vincent's finest portrait of a peasant was painted at Arles. Vincent's Provençal landscapes – cherry orchards, vineyards, olive groves, cornfields, etc – provide a fairly complete picture of the intensive cultivation typical of the region in the late nineteenth century. A comparison of Vincent's *'Harvest'*, a view of the plain of La Crau executed in 1888, with a photograph of the same area taken in the 1960s reveals that a dramatic decline has taken place in agriculture since Vincent's day.

Vincent had various reasons for his selection of Provence as a site for a Studio in the South. Amongst them was the reputed beauty of the Arlésiennes. This was one of the selling points Vincent used to persuade Gauguin to join him in Arles. Gauguin described the Arlésiennes as follows: *"The women here have elegant head-dresses and a Greek beauty. Their shawls fall into folds as in primitive paintings . . . Well, it is worth studying. In any event, here is a source of beautiful **modern style**"*.[15] Here we encounter the paradox that modernity in art is to be based on the ancient and the primitive.

Patience Escalier

One critic has described Vincent's painting *'Peasant from the Camargue: Patience Escalier'* (1888) as *'the only great portrait of a peasant in the history of art'*. In a letter from Arles Vincent informed Theo: *"You are shortly to make the acquaintance of Master Patience Escalier, a sort of 'man with a hoe', (Millet's famous painting) formerly cowherd of the Camargue, now a gardener at a house in the Crau (a plain near Arles). The colouring of this peasant portrait is not so black as in 'Potato eaters' of Nuenen, but our highly civilized Parisian* ***Portier*** *(A. Portier was a Paris art dealer) – probably so-called because he chucks pictures out – will be bothered by the same old problems. You have changed since then, but you will see* ***he*** *has not, and it really is a pity that there are not more pictures* ***en sabots*** *in Paris. I do not think that my peasant would do any harm to the de Lautrec in your possession if they were hung side by side, and I am bold enough to hope the de Lautrec would appear more distinguished by the mutual contrast, and that on the other hand my picture would gain by the odd juxtaposition, because that sun-steeped, sunburned quality, tanned and air-swept, would show up still more effectively beside all that face powder and elegance"*. (The Lautrec is almost certainly *'Young woman sitting at a table'* also called *'Poudre de riz'* oil on canvas, 56 x 46 cm).[16]

It is clear from the above that Vincent conceived of his peasant portrait as one half of a montage juxtaposition involving the rhetorical device of antithesis, the opposed terms of which were rural/urban, rude/sophisticated, male/female, outdoor/indoor.

Town and country

Notwithstanding Vincent's emotional identification with miners, weavers and poor peasants he could not find a permanent home amongst them. Unlike Millet, who was born a peasant and always felt himself to be one, Vincent remained an outsider as far as peasants were concerned. Having learnt all he could from the city Millet returned to the countryside and planted himself there for the rest of his life. In contrast, Vincent could not settle down anywhere for more than a short period of time; he was even more of a wanderer than Courbet. His various professions caused him to shift his place of abode from Holland to England, to Belgium and to France; he also moved around within those countries. In short, Vincent was a restless, rootless intellectual who could not find a satisfactory nest anywhere (bird's nests attracted him as a motif for this very reason).

Carl Nordenfalk observes that *"Van Gogh's whole career is characterized by an oscillation between town and country"*.[17] Both had their particular characteristics, their attractions and drawbacks. Vincent was pulled from one to the other: in the city he longed for contact with Nature and simple folk; in the country he longed for contact with Art, Culture and intellectuals. Vincent's rootlessness was not due to some problem of personality unique to him, rather it was symptomatic of a much broader problem, namely, the antithesis of town and country. As Frederick Engels explains: *"The first great division of labour, the separation of town and country, condemned the rural population to thousands of years of mental torpidity, and the people of the towns each to subjection to his own individual trade. It destroyed the basis of the intellectual development of the former and the physical development of the latter. When the peasant appropriates his land, and the townsman his trade, his land appropriates the peasant and his trade the townsman to the very same extent. In the division of labour, man is also divided. All other physical and mental faculties are sacrificed to the development of one single activity"*.[18]

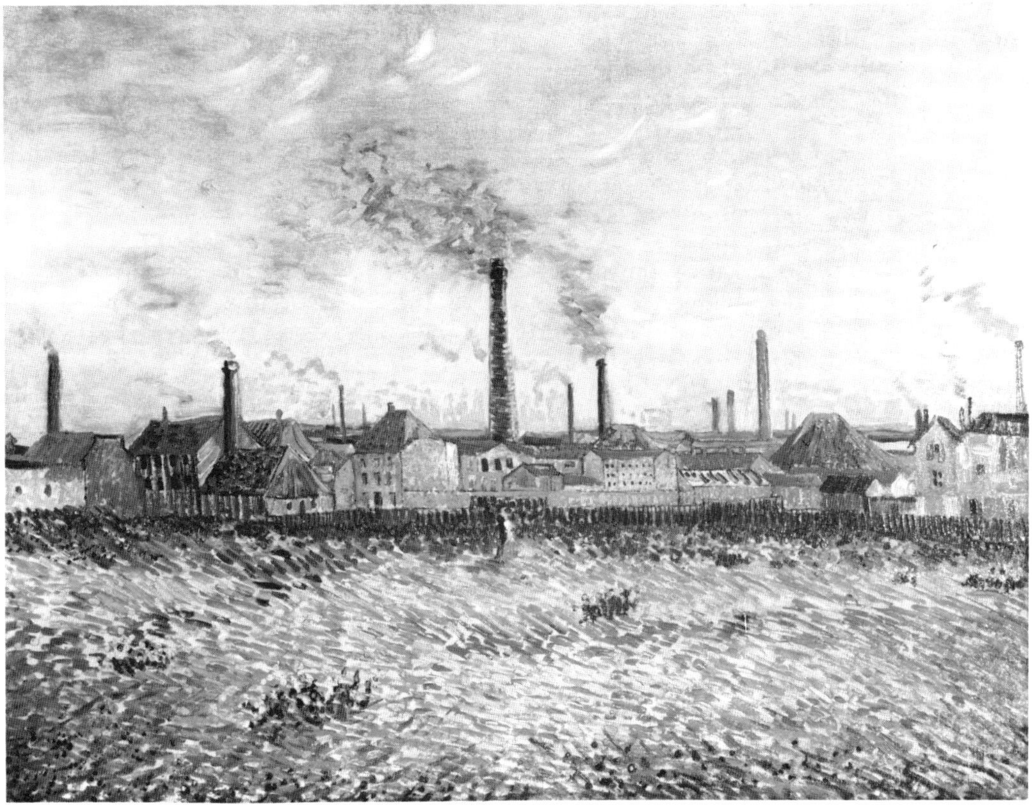

(73) *The Huth factories at Clichy,* Paris 1887, oil on canvas, 53.9 x 71.9 cm, St Louis Art Museum.

(74) *The old peasant Patience Escalier,* Arles 1888, oil on canvas, 69 x 56 cm, Private collection.

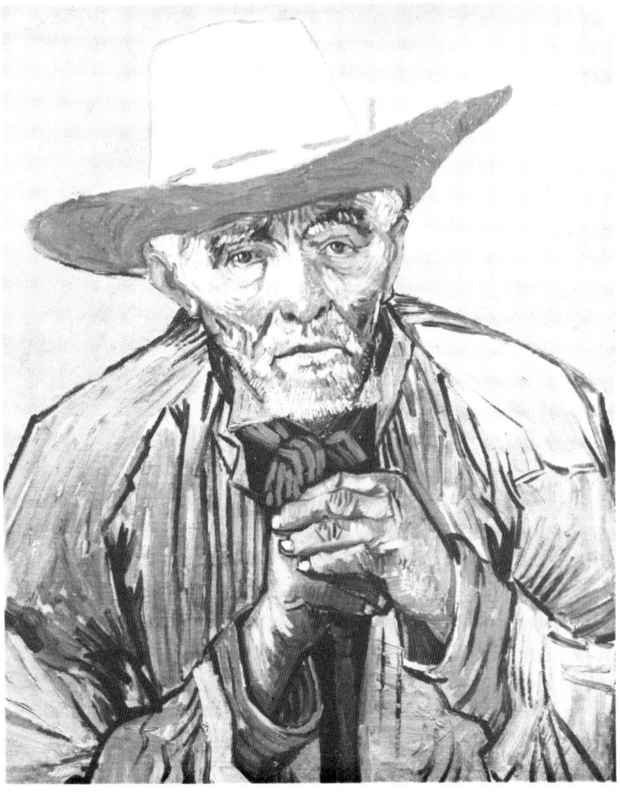

Vincent was almost certainly unaware of this type of Marxist theoretical analysis but he was surely aware of the dichotomy between the urban and the rural, industry and agriculture, proletariat and peasantry. While at Paris, and later at Arles, he documented the growth of suburbs, and he carried his easel into the fields adjoining the town and then looking back he recorded the profile of the town against the sky with its ever-increasing number of factory chimneys. These images derive from the very boundary line dividing the urban and the rural; they seem to be pictorial musings on the contradictions of town and country during the late nineteenth century.

He must also have been aware of how, as a result of the division of labour and increasing specialization, human beings were developing one-sidedly whether they were miners, weavers, peasants, or painters, and how the gap between mental and manual labour was becoming wider and wider.

'The sower' and 'The reaper'

Vincent once remarked to Theo that Millet was more of a father to him than his real father. Some of the first drawings Vincent made were paraphrases of Millet's *'The sower'* and *'Diggers'*. An examination of Millet's *'Sower'* picture reveals a biblical reference and a sexual/artistic creation metaphor. Both these aspects are applicable to Vincent's numerous depictions of sowers. *"Painting"*, Vincent observed, *"is sometimes sowing, though the painter may not reap"*. Taken together his pictures *'The sower'* and *'The reaper'*, painted at Arles and St. Rémy respectively, are images of the act of conception and of death. In fact, Vincent produced two major works on the theme of the sower at Arles, one painted in June 1888 and the other in October 1888. The first painting is an extremely powerful image: Vincent looks directly towards the large yellow orb of the setting sun; the sky consists of intense yellows and greens, the earth violets and oranges. Optical flicker caused by the juxtaposition of saturated colours different in hue but similar in tone produces a sensation of dazzle in the eyes of the spectator comparable to that caused by the sun itself.

As Vincent explained to Theo, his intention was to do Millet – whose pictures he found too grey – over again in colour. Vincent's picture is organized in terms of binary oppositions: the space is divided into two parts – heaven and earth – by means of a horizon line; the primary clash of colours is between yellow (the sky) and violet (the earth). The figure of the sower, placed asymmetrically on the right, bridges the division between heaven and earth. For Vincent the world was ruled by positive and negative forces: the struggle between good and evil, light and dark, neither of which could exist without the other. Similarly, he always used colour in terms of pairs, that is, complementaries; he equated them with masculinity and feminity saying that complementaries enhanced and completed one another like men and women. If we recall the biblical reference – the field is a metaphor for the world, the wheat a metaphor for humanity – then the sower combines both positive and negative forces: he sows the good seeds and the tares. And the sower, the creator, is also the artist: the sower's arm and Vincent's signature are aligned along the same diagonal.

As H. R. Graetz explains: *"The sower strewing seed thus sows the wheat – the image of humanity. This makes him a potent symbol of creation in the work of Vincent who* ***ploughed on his canvases like the peasants on their fields.*** *The* ***real life*** *with a wife and children has been denied him* ***"And if one is frustrated physically in this power, one tries to create thoughts instead of children, thus one is nevertheless part of humanity"****. . . the 'Sower' is one of Vincent's most outstanding self-portrayals, symbolic of the core of his life, his spiritual struggle against what he called physical frustration . . . His* ***cutting the painting in two*** *confirms the symptomatic conflict between the opposing forces of dark and light, of negative and positive within him".*[19]

The October version of *'The sower'* owes more to Japanese prints than it does to Millet: its composition is much more two-dimensional; a dark sower and a dark tree trunk lie on the surface plane of the canvas silhouetted against the distant landscape; the tree trunk cuts across the whole picture from bottom edge to top edge. Graetz interprets the tree as a symbol of struggle, the horizon as a line of life, and the sun as a symbol of love and light. The horizon, or life line, cuts through the head of the sower. His head is framed by the enormous golden disc of the sun built up from thick slabs of yellow pigment. In other words, Vincent finds a natural means of endowing the sower with a saint's halo. In this way Vincent is able to incorporate religious meaning without depicting scenes from the Bible.

As a result of a mental breakdown Vincent spent the period from May 1889 to May 1890 in an asylum at St. Rémy. From the window of his cell on the first floor Vincent could see a walled garden beyond which were the foothills of the Alps. He drew and painted this view many times but he always left out the iron bars of his cell window. In reference to his painting of a reaper at work in the asylum garden Vincent wrote: *I saw then in this reaper – a vague figure struggling like a devil in great heat to come to the end of his task – I saw then in it the image of death, in the sense that humanity would be the wheat one reaps. So it is, if you like, the opposite of that sower I tried before".*[20] Just as Vincent identified himself with the sower so he identified himself with the reaper: like the reaper he too was struggling to complete a task. But he also recognised that he was part of the wheat; in a letter to his sister he wrote: *"are'nt we, who live on bread, ourselves wheat to a considerable extent, at least should we not submit to growing without the power to move like a plant . . . and to be mown like it when we are ripe".*[21]

In such pictures we are a long way from the prosaic reality of peasant existence, a long way from the empiricism of Courbet. Vincent subjectivizes the objective world by imbuing it with his own feelings about life and death, and by representing it in terms of ancient biblical metaphors.

Art and religion

In sharp contrast to Courbet who was an atheist and an anti-cleric, Millet and van Gogh were profoundly influenced by religion. Millet's family included curés and Catholicism was a dominant influence on his upbringing. According to some authorities he eventually became an agnostic but even so much of his work exudes religiosity. Van Gogh was strongly influenced by Protestantism: his father was a pastor serving the Dutch reformed Church and Vincent himself worked for a period as a preacher and as a missionary.

Art has a relative autonomy; so do religious ideologies; the problem for the art historian is to show how a particular religious ideology is refracted through its representation in a work of art. In the case of Millet and van Gogh the challenge would be to explain how Millet's peasant paintings related to the Catholicism of his day and how van Gogh's related to the Protestantism of his day.[22] Such a comparative project would require a great deal of research therefore I will confine myself here to some general remarks applicable to both artists.

Christianity is a politically conservative force in so far as it teaches a meek acceptance of the existing social order ('render unto Caesar' etc). Millet did not believe that social progress was possible; van Gogh hoped for it but his pictures reveal nothing but pessimism. Neither artist's depictions of peasants give any sign that the peasantry has the capacity to rebel against oppression even though history is full of examples

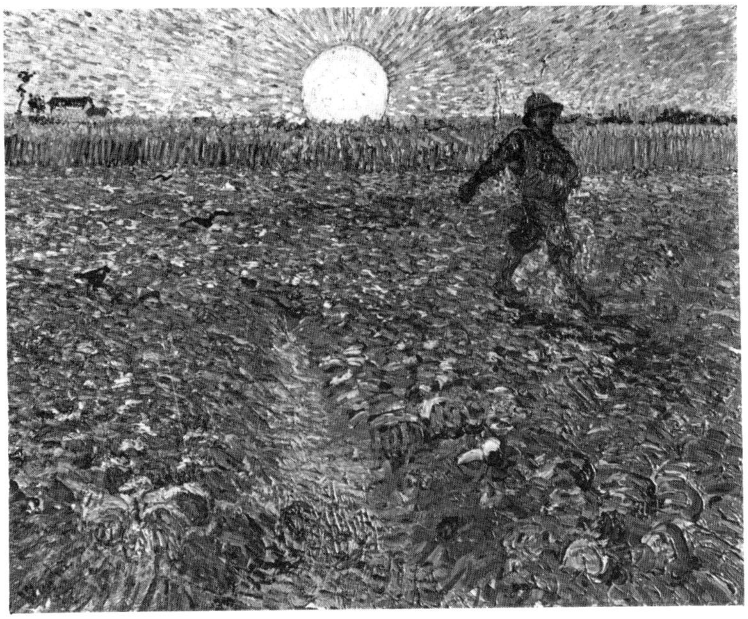

(75) *Sower with setting sun,* Arles 1888, oil on canvas, 64 x 80.5 cm, Otterlo, Rijksmuseum Kröller-Müller.

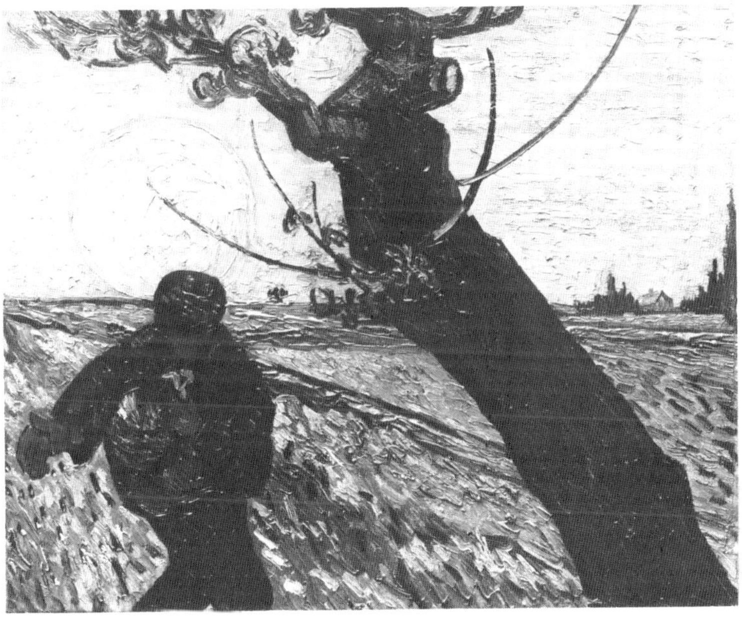

(76) *Sower with setting sun,* Arles 1888, oil on canvas, 32 x 40 cm, Amsterdam, Rijksmuseum Vincent van Gogh.

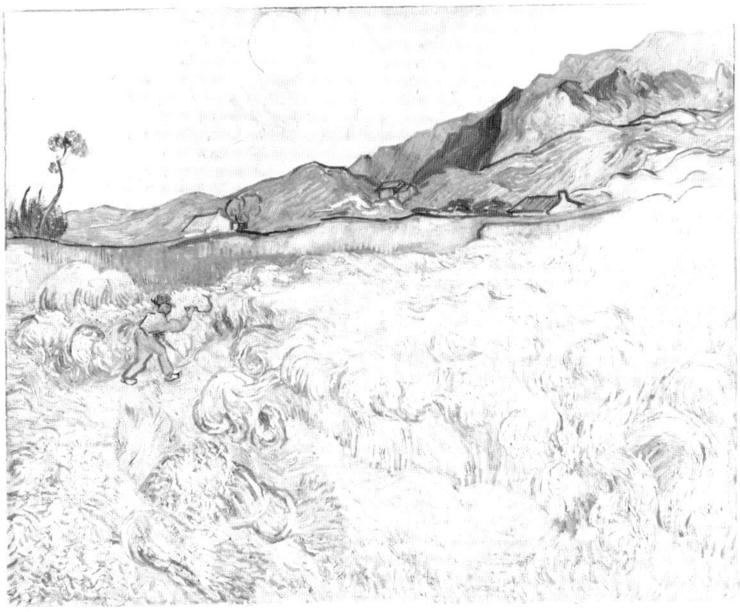

(77) *Enclosed field with reaper at sunrise,* St Rémy 1889, oil on canvas, 74 x 92 cm, Amsterdam, Rijksmuseum Vincent van Gogh.

of revolts by the peasantry; neither artist shows peasants organizing themselves or struggling politically. All they show are peasants weighed down by labour, crushed by circumstances, fixed in place at the bottom of the social hierarchy. The implicit moral of their peasant paintings is therefore: 'these things are eternal, no change is possible, nothing can be done'; in short, a philosophy of acceptance, quietism, defeatism. The only recompense for man's suffering is in the next world not in this one.

Millet once executed a work for the Pope on the subject of the immaculate conception but as a rule he avoided explicitly religious or biblical themes. Christianity was, rather, implicit in his paintings; it was there as a 'hidden' symbolism. Similarly, van Gogh avoided, for the most part, traditional religious subjects: his aim was to express religious sentiments by combining complementary colours. The fact is that by the nineteenth century religious art had lost all its former conviction because the age was becoming increasingly secular and profane; had not Nietzsche announced in 1882 *'God is dead'*? Since it was no longer possible to employ Christian iconography directly, those artists who remained attached to Christianity had to find some indirect manner of incorporating it into their art. At all events it was a backward looking phenomenon. Millet's and van Gogh's peasant paintings were a manifestation of what George Lichtheim terms *'agarian romanticism'*, a looking backwards in order to repudiate the modern world of industry and cities.[23]

What was radical about van Gogh's work was not his subject matter but his artistic innovations, his formal innovations (intense saturated colours, exaggerated perspectives, emphatic brushstrokes, thick paint, expressionism, etc). In van Gogh's case, therefore, artistic radicalism was not aligned with political radicalism. Both artists identified with the peasants as personifications of suffering humanity; the limit of their political ambition was to arouse the social conscience of the art public of the city to the plight of the poor peasantry.

For Marx the idea that God made mankind was an inversion of the truth because *"Man makes religion, religion does not make man"*. On the one hand religion embodies the highest aspirations of the human species while on the other it obscures the real conditions that it is necessary to change if those aspirations are to be fulfilled in reality rather than in imagination or in the next world: *"**Religious** suffering is at one and the same time the expression of real suffering and a protest against real suffering. Religion is the sigh of the oppressed creature, the heart of a heartless world and the soul of the souless conditions. It is the **opium** of the people. The abolition of religion as the **illusory** happiness of the people is the demand for their real happiness. To call on them to give up their illusions about their conditions is to **call on them to give up a condition that requires illusions**. The criticism of religion is therefore in **embryo** the **criticism of that vale of tears** of which religion is the **halo**".*[24]

Neither Millet nor van Gogh were capable of this degree of understanding. They recognised suffering and they recognised religion as a consolation for that suffering but instead of criticising the halo they reproduced it. Nevertheless, the fact that they both deified workers and poor peasants (rather than depicting Biblical personages) and the fact that they unified spirit and nature indicated a movement within their thinking towards Marx's position. But we have to turn to the work of Courbet to find images of peasants without biblical overtones, to find pictorial attacks on the Christian religion.

Notes and references:

1. Quotations from van Gogh's letters are from *The complete letters of Vincent van Gogh* (Thames & Hudson, 1958). Letter 194.

2. J. Meier-Graefe 'Vincent and socialism' *Van Gogh in perspective*; ed by B. Welsh-Ovcharov (Engelwood Cliffs, NJ : Prentice-Hall, 1974) pp 72–77.

3. Letter 379.

4. see *English influences on Vincent van Gogh* (Nottingham : Fine Art Dept of Nottingham University/ Arts Council, 1974).

5. Letter 240.

6. Letter 245.

7. Letter 398.

8. F. Novotny 'Reflections on a drawing by van Gogh' *Art bulletin* 35(1) March 1953 pp 35–43.

9. Letter 411.

10. K. Marx 'The eighteenth Brumaire of Louis Bonaparte' *Surveys from exile* (Penguin Books, 1973) p 239.

11. Letter 404.

12. C. Nordenfalk 'Van Gogh and literature' *Journal of the Warburg and Courtauld Institutes* 10 1947 pp 132–47.

13. Letter 129.

14. Letter 130.

15. W. Andersen *Gauguin's paradise lost* (Secker and Warburg, 1972) p 8.

16. Letter from G. Heuff, Rijksmuseum Vincent van Gogh.

17. *The life and work of van Gogh* (Elek. 1953).

18. F. Engels *Anti-Dühring* (Lawrence & Wishart, 1973) p 346.

19. H. R. Graetz *The symbolic language of van Gogh* (Thames & Hudson, 1963) p 101.

20. Letter 604.

21. Letter 13 (to Wilhelmina).

22. Some authorities on Millet claim that he was an agnostic; it could be argued that the Catholicism of his paintings is that of his depicted characters rather than his own personal beliefs.

23. G. Lichtheim *A short history of socialism* (Fontana/ Collins, 1975).

24. K. Marx 'A contribution to the critique of Hegel's philosophy of right' *Early writings* (Penguin Books, 1975) p 244.

ART HISTORY VERSUS PHILOSOPHY

THE ENIGMA OF THE 'OLD SHOES'

This paper is an account of, and a contribution to, a dispute between a number of scholars from various disciplines about the meaning of a painting depicting two old shoes executed by Vincent van Gogh in the 1880s. The painting has been interpreted differently by different scholars in the years since it was produced, hence what we are concerned with here is its reception through time. (This paper is, therefore, a contribution to what is called 'reception history'.)[1] To some readers it may seem that a remarkable amount of fuss is being made about a trivial matter, yet in the course of this theoretical debate fundamental issues concerning the nature of art and truth, the mechanisms of signs, and the methodology of art history are raised. As I hope to show, in the last resort the battle for the meaning of the van Gogh painting is a political struggle.

At the outset it is necessary to give a chronology of the events leading to the present situation:

1884–85 At Nuenen, Holland, Vincent van Gogh painted still-life pictures including,amongst the objects depicted,pairs of wooden clogs or sabots.

1886–7 In Paris Vincent painted a series of pictures of old shoes and boots. Later in Arles in 1888 he painted two more pictures of old shoes and sabots.

1930 In Amsterdam,in March,the German philosopher Martin Heidegger saw two of Vincent's shoe paintings in an exhibition. Between 1930 and 1935 Heidegger wrote an essay entitled *'The origin of the work of art'* first delivered as a lecture in Freiberg in February 1935 in which he gave a poetic interpretation of one of van Gogh's shoe paintings.[2]

1968 In New York the noted American art historian Meyer Schapiro published a short essay entitled *'The still life as a personal object – a note on Heidegger and van Gogh'* in which he disputed the interpretation forwarded by Heidegger.[3]

1978 In Paris the art theory magazine *Macula* published the texts of Heidegger's essay and Schapiro's response plus a playful, punning essay by the French philosopher Jacques Derrida in which Schapiro is found guilty of *'pre-critical naivety'* and *'dogmatism'*.[4]

1979 In Paris the art magazine *Opus international* published an article by Pierre Taguiev in which the history of the debate is reviewed and the author adds further reflections of his own.[5]

Let us begin by examining Heidegger's reception of the *'Old shoes'* painting.

Although Heidegger's essay is a lengthy one, the section describing the van Gogh painting is quite short. Here it is:

"As long as we only imagine a pair of shoes in general, or simply look at the empty, unused shoes as they merely stand there in the picture, we shall never discover what the equipmental being of the equipment in truth is. From van Gogh's painting we cannot even tell where these shoes stand. There is nothing surrounding this pair of peasant shoes in or to which they might belong–only an undefined space. There are not even clods of soil from the field or the field-path sticking to them, which would at least hint at their use. A pair of peasant shoes and nothing more. And yet–

From the dark opening of the worn insides of the shoes the toilsome tread of the worker stares forth. In the stiffly rugged heaviness of the shoes there is the accumulated tenacity of her slow trudge through the far-spreading and ever-uniform furrows of the field swept by a raw wind. On the leather lie the dampness and richness of the soil. Under the soles slides the loneliness of the field-path as evening falls. In the shoes vibrates the silent call of the earth, its quiet gift of the ripening grain and its unexplained self-refusal in the fallow desolation of the wintry field. This equipment is pervaded by uncomplaining anxiety as to the certainty of bread, the wordless joy of having once more withstood want, the trembling before the impending childbed and shivering at the surrounding meance of death. This equipment belongs to the earth, and it is protected in the world of the peasant woman. From out of this protected belonging the equipment itself rises to its resting-within-itself".[6]

(Derrida makes the valid point that one of Schapiro's criticisms of Heidegger – that he extracts one painting of shoes from a series of such paintings and discusses it in isolation – applies equally to Schapiro's own method – he extracts a passage from a long essay by Heidegger and discusses it without considering its relationship to the essay as a whole.)

Heidegger cites the van Gogh painting while attempting to discover the equipmentality of

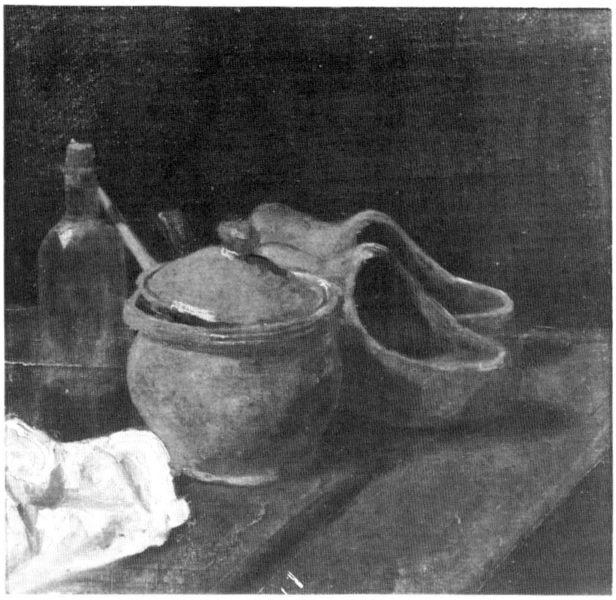

(78) *Still life with earthen pot and clogs,* Nuenen 1885, oil on canvas on panel, 39 x 41.5 cm, Otterlo, Rijksmuseum Kröller-Müller.

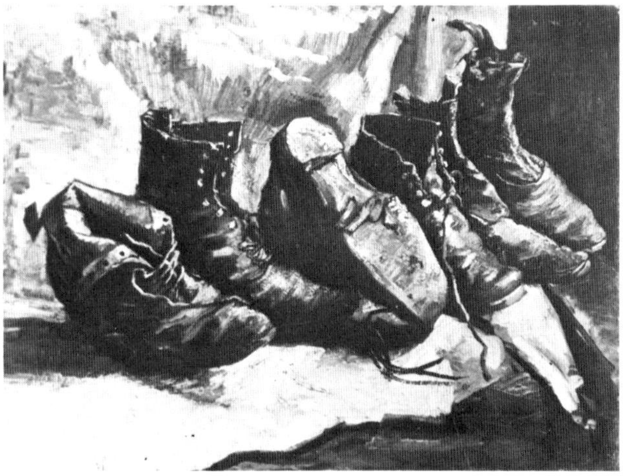

(80) *Three pairs of shoes, one shoe upsidedown,* Paris 1887, oil on canvas, 49 x 72 cm, Cambridge (Mass), Fogg Art Museum Harvard University.

equipment (tools, utensils, etc), the *being* of shoes; that is, his intention is not to analyse the painting in the manner of an art critic or an art historian. His response to the picture is a kind of reverie prompted by the sight of a pair of old shoes. Heidegger comments on the way van Gogh presents the shoes against an undefined, indeterminate background, but otherwise his response refers to shoes as if he were studying real shoes rather than a painted image of shoes. The philosopher was obviously aware of this point because he immediately adds: *"But perhaps it is only in the picture that we notice all this about the shoes".* The implication here is that the painting provides a way of seeing a pair of shoes which would be unavailable to us in everyday perception. I will return to this point later.

Generally speaking, Heidegger does not employ

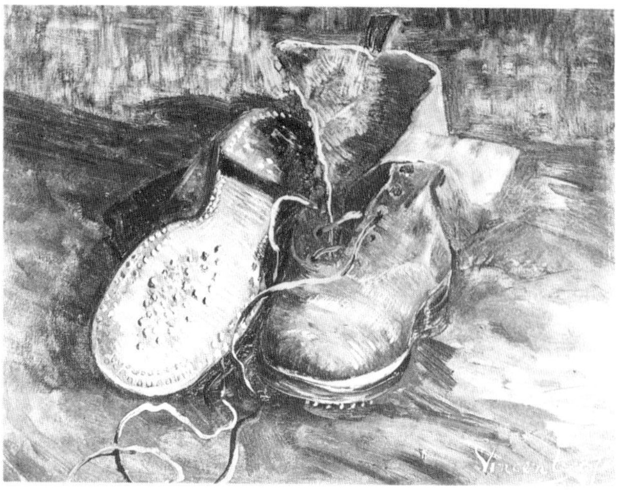

(79) *A pair of shoes, one upsidedown,* Paris 1887, oil on canvas, 34 x 41.5, Baltimore Museum of Art.

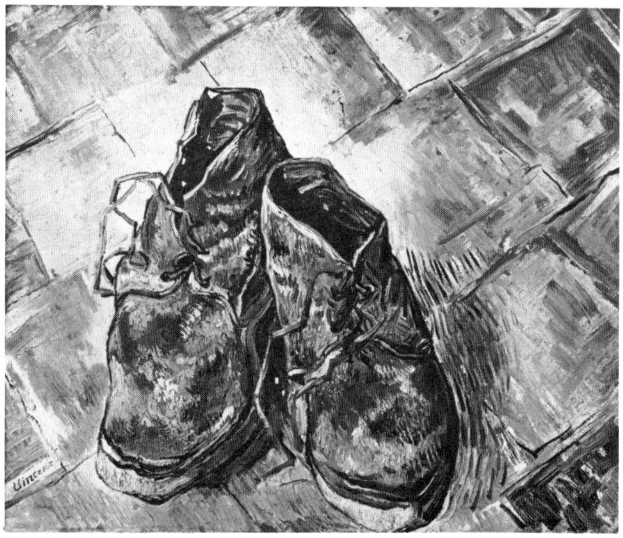

(81) *A pair of old shoes,* Arles 1888, oil on canvas, 44 x 53 cm, New York, Private collection.

the specialist vocabulary of his profession, instead he uses everyday words in technical, specialist or private ways, for example, the words 'earth' and 'world' have particular meanings within his writings. It is exceedingly difficult to take issue with a part of his work, as I am attempting to do here, because all his concepts are interrelated and interdependent. Consequently, his philosophy presents us with an all or nothing choice.

Thus far I have been referring to 'a *pair* of shoes'. Before continuing I should add that Derrida throws doubt on even this commonsense assumption by arguing that we cannot be certain it is 'a pair' of shoes which are represented since it could be two right shoes or two left shoes. I think in this instance scepticism is being taken to absurd extremes.

Which painting did Heidegger mean?

It is entirely typical of the philosophy of

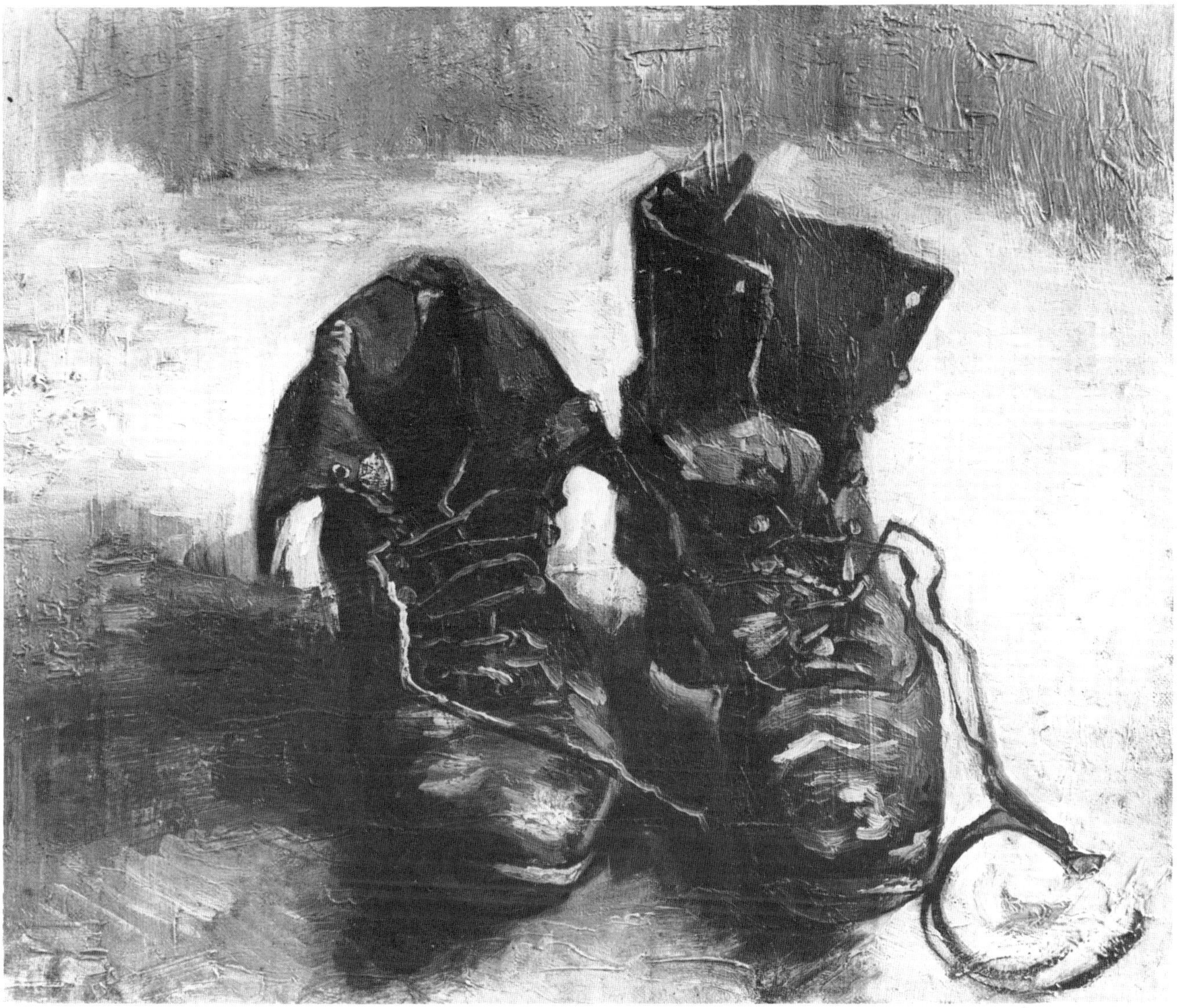

(82) *A pair of old shoes,* Paris 1886, oil on canvas, 37.5 x 45.5 cm, Amsterdam, Rijksmuseum Vincent van Gogh.

Heidegger that he does not specify exactly which painting by van Gogh he is referring to. Such concrete particulars, such mundane details, are beneath the philosopher's attention, preoccupied as he is with such lofty and nebulous general concepts as Being and Time. As Schapiro points out, Heidegger was aware that van Gogh painted the shoe motif several times *"but he does not identify the picture he has in mind, as if the different versions are interchangeable, all presenting the same truth".* In an attempt to settle this point Schapiro wrote to Heidegger in 1965 and was told that the painting in question had been seen in an exhibition held in Amsterdam in 1930. Schapiro then checked up on that exhibition's contents and discovered that two paintings of shoes had been included but there was only one – *'Old shoes'* (De la Faille 255) – which corresponded to Heidegger's description. We can be reasonably certain, therefore, that this painting is the one Heidegger had in mind when writing *'The origin of the work of art*.

Heidegger shows no interest in when or where the van Gogh was painted. In other words, he is indifferent to the precise social and historical circumstances in which it was produced even though such circumstances are, from the art historian's point of view, crucial to any consideration of the work's meaning. The social context is crucial because every work of art is a partial statement which cannot contain within its frame all the information needed for its comprehension. The historical moment is crucial because as time passes society changes and so do the meanings attributed to works of art. Heidegger is also indifferent to the relationship between the *'Old shoes'* picture and the rest of van Gogh's oeuvre and to its relationship to other works on the same theme by other artists. These factors are relevant to an understanding of the picture's meaning.

The question of ownership: who did the shoes belong to?

In his lyrical response to van Gogh's painting Heidegger makes two unwarranted assumptions: firstly, he assumes that the shoes are those of a peasant; and secondly, that they are those of a female. There is no pictorial evidence to support either of these contentions and Schapiro is surely right to criticize Heidegger for *projecting* this information on to the picture. If Heidegger had been interested in the actual condition of the Dutch peasantry in the 1880s and van Gogh's work as a systematic documentation of that historical reality he would have examined other paintings and drawings of Dutch peasants by van Gogh to see what they normally wore on their feet. He would then have discovered that they wore *wooden clogs* not leather shoes. If van Gogh's images are accepted as accurate depictions then we are justified in concluding that the Dutch peasantry was too poor to be able to afford leather shoes. A concern with concrete material reality, with the lived experience of real human beings is, however, of no interest to the philosopher Heidegger. Of course, my objections to Heidegger are based on a correspondence theory of truth, that is, I assume there is a degree of homology between the pictorial statements and the state of the world at a given time, and it must be admitted that Heidegger rejects this conception of truth.

Why Heidegger ascribes a female gender to the shoes is a mystery. (Schapiro, as Derrida points out, pays little attention to this problem: Schapiro is convinced the shoes are Vincent's consequently it seems obvious to him that they are men's shoes.) Derrida suggests that Heidegger may have been influenced by the many portraits of female peasants in van Gogh's oeuvre. This is a plausible explanation but the matter cannot be investigated further because of a lack of information. (It will be argued here that the shoes are those of a man. This argument is based on a consideration of the types of shoes depicted in the set of shoe-paintings executed in Paris.)

Assuming then that the shoes did not belong to a female peasant, who did they belong to? The painting is haunted by an absence, a ghost, i.e. the missing owner. (This is why Derrida talks about 'restitution'. the attempt by art historians to restore the shoes to their correct owner.) I will return to this problem shortly.

Not only does Heidegger ignore the evidence supplied by other works by van Gogh he rejects in toto the discipline of art history as a means of experiencing works of art: *"Art-historical study makes the works the objects of a science. Yet in all this busy activity do we encounter the work itself?"*.[7] Heidegger's argument is that the world to which the work of art was originally related has disappeared, a painting viewed in an exhibition is detached from its original context, hence there is no point in the art historian reconstructing it. *"The work now belongs"*, he asserts, *"as work, uniquely within the realm that is opened up by itself"*. In other words, the *work* of the work of art creates a space, an opening, makes visible, makes present a world, in this instance the world of a peasant woman, which is then as it were projected into the future. Heidegger's objection to art history appears to be that its practitioners are concerned with the external relations of the work and its meaning/significance at the time it was made and not with the work itself as experienced in present time by a living human being who in seeing it re-creates its meaning. The implication here is that there is no original, true meaning to the work determined by historical and social context or by artistic intention but a whole series of meanings or readings which are valid in terms of the viewer's experience. It would seem that for Heidegger it is impossible to *mis*read a work of art, consequently we must not expect any admission from him that the van Gogh was misinterpreted.

Does this commit us to a relativistic, pluralistic situation in which all and any interpretations of a picture are valid? Is it not possible to judge that one interpretation is false and another is true, or that at least some interpretations are more convincing and plausible than others?

Heidegger's contention is that the work of art is detached from its socio-historical context. This tactic enables him to dismiss as irrelevant the whole apparatus of art history and leaves him free to concentrate all his attention on the work itself. A work of art does indeed have a relative autonomy and may survive long after the epoch in which it was made, nevertheless every work of art is an *historical* product and is, therefore, marked by the era of which it was a part. Of course, as time passes the work changes, society changes; even so something of its historicity remains embedded in its very fabric. By detaching the painting in the way that he does, Heidegger hopes to avoid awkward questions about the ideological, political and social functions of art in a given society; (he shows no interest in the nineteenth centry audience for whom artists like van Gogh were working). If his own philosophy was similarly detached from the German culture of the 1920s and 1930s no awkward questions could be asked about the social implications of his writings or about his flirtation with Nazism.

Heidegger seems to think that all that is needed to comprehend a work of art is supplied by the work of art in question. This ignores all the memories, knowledge, and associations, which the viewer brings to the work of art (what Gombrich calls 'the beholder's share'). No viewer approaches a work of art with a blank or empty mind. No viewer could even recognise an image of shoes without previous knowledge of shoes. The artifact is only *part* of the work of art. And the more knowledge the viewer possesses in relation to the work of art – knowledge of techniques, materials and conventions of painting, of the subject matter, of the artist, of the social context, etc – the richer will be his or her understanding and appreciation of the work of art.

Schapiro is reproached by the French defenders of Heidegger for reducing the truth of the van Gogh painting to a date, a title, a number in a catalogue raisonné. He is accused of positivism. What is being placed in question here are the standard techniques of art history as a discipline, in particular those of connoisseurship (that is, determining authorship and date), which Schapiro invokes because he is a professional art historian. Heidegger explicitly rejects these art historical practices as useless for the understanding of a picture. Let us acknowledge that there is much more to a painting than its authorship, title and date, but even so Heidegger, and Schapiro's critics, overlook the fact that the vast majority of titles are supplied by artists and that in many instances artists date and sign their canvases. (The *'Old shoes'* painting has a signature 'Vincent' in the top left-hand corner; it is not dated but another in the same series is dated '87'.) When, therefore, dates, signatures and titles have been supplied by the artist they are integral parts of the work of art and consequently it is perfectly legitimate for the art historian to take them into account in any interpretation of the painting.

Schapiro has two principal objections to Heidegger's interpretation of the *'Old shoes'* picture: firstly, the philosopher has wrongly identified the owner of the shoes; secondly, the philosopher treats the painting as if it were a window on the world, that is, Heidegger's response to the picture is no different than if he viewed a pair of shoes directly. One would have expected Schapiro to elaborate on the difference between the direct perception of a pair of shoes and the perception of a pictorial representation of a pair of shoes but this does not happen. Instead Schapiro claims that Heidegger's oversight was to ignore *"the personal and physiognomic in the shoes"*, that is, their special significance to van Gogh. Schapiro makes the assumption that the shoes belonged to van Gogh even though there is no evidence in the picture to confirm this, and he interprets the shoes picture as a self-portrait, as an expression of Vincent's private self. But surely this interpretation is little better than Heidegger's because firstly it makes an assumption of ownership which cannot be proved and secondly, it still conflates the real shoes with their pictorial representation.

Literary analogies and sources

It is interesting to note that in order to justify his interpretation of the *'Old shoes'* painting Schapiro resorts to a literary analogy. He quotes from the novel *Hunger* written by the Norwegian Knut Hamsum in the 1880s in which the author self-consciously studies a pair of his own shoes as a means of understanding his own personality. Schapiro's choice of text was unfortunate because, as Leo Lowenthal showed in his 1937 critique of Hamsun's novels, there was a significant correlation between the novelist's *Volkish* themes and authoritarian attitudes and those of Nazi ideology.[8] (The validity of Lowenthal's analysis was confirmed by Hamsum's collaboration with the Nazis in World War two.)

Let us consider the question of ownership further. Schapiro's assertion that the shoes were those of van Gogh is a reasonable supposition given the known facts about his life but the matter cannot be established with absolute certainty; the shoes could have belonged to Theo or to other friends and acquaintances. H. R. Graetz, author of a book *The symbolic language of van Gogh* which adopts a psychological approach to the paintings, agrees with Schapiro the shoes stand for the wearer and can serve therefore as a portrait of the owner.[9] However, Graetz not only identifies the shoes with Vincent but also with Theo, that is, he sees the two shoes as symbolizing the symbiotic relationship between the two brothers. The more downtrodden shoe on the left he equates with Vincent and the more upright one on the right with Theo. The lace reaching over from the left shoe to the right he sees as a kind of umbilical cord linking Vincent to Theo! Again, in view of the facts of van Gogh's life, Graetz's theory is a plausible one but there appears to be no means of testing its validity.[10]

Faced by the limited information provided by pictures the art historian's instinct (unlike the philosopher's) is to seek additional information from other sources, generally speaking written documents of various kinds (in other words, the philological method). Van Gogh scholars are fortunate in this respect because of the hundreds of letters he wrote to his brother Theo but not of course while he lived with Theo in Paris. Our knowledge of the Paris period is therefore hindered by the lack of letters, nevertheless many of those who met Vincent have left reminiscences. For example, Francois Gauzi (1861–1933), a fellow student of van Gogh at Cormon's studio, recounts this anecdote concerning a visit to the van Gogh apartment: *"Just then he was finishing a still-life which he showed to me. He had purchased at the flea market a pair of old, worn-out shoes, shoes of a street pedlar which nonetheless were clean and freshly polished. They were sturdy footwear lacking in fantasy. He put on these shoes one rainy afternoon and took a walk along the fortifications. Covered with mud, they appeared more interesting. A study is not necessarily a painting; army boots or roses might have served just as well. Vincent copies his pair of shoes faithfully. This idea, which was hardly revolutionary, appeared bizarre to some of us, his studio comrades, who could not imagine a plate of apples hanging in a dining room as a companion piece to a pair of hobnailed boots".*[11] (It is frustrating to note that even from this description we cannot be sure which of van Gogh's shoe paintings Gauzi saw.)

Gauzi calls the shoe paintings 'studies' meaning exercises done in order to improve technique, to keep in practice, or as a step towards a larger, more ambitious work. During his stay in Paris van Gogh did indeed undertake many studies in order to experiment with colour combinations and with brush techniques but the shoe paintings appear to have been more than merely studies for van Gogh. By painting extremely humble subjects such as piles of potatoes and old shoes van Gogh challenged the limits of the genre of still-life painting and also the taste of the bourgeois art public. Most art collectors of that period would indeed have found the subject matter and vigour of handling of the shoe pictures inappropriate as decorations for the walls of their sitting or dining rooms.

From Vincent's letters to Theo and his artist friends we know that he read many books and that his paintings were often directly influenced by literary images and ideas.[12] In March 1883 Vincent wrote to van Rappard telling him that he was reading Thomas Carlyle's *Sartor resartus* (Carlyle [1795–1889], social critic and Tory Romanticist, was a favourite writer of van Gogh despite the fact that he always expressed indifference or even hostility towards the visual arts) and described it as *'the philosophy of old clothes'.* Carlyle's book contains passages in which empty and old clothes are celebrated as *"the shells and outer husks of the body . . . as the pure emblem and effigies of man".*[13] Man can be revered via his empty and old clothes, argues Carlyle, because the form and image of man is retained without the flesh which is subject to *"devilish passion".* The notion of a portrait of humanity even though that humanity is literally absent from the scene corresponds exactly to the way in which Vincent's shoe paintings work. I think we can assume, therefore, that Carlyle's views on old clothes were not far from Vincent's mind when he painted the shoe series.

Indeed, there are parts of *Sartor resartus* which could almost serve as theoretical explanations of Vincent's artistic practice; for example, Carlyle regards clothes as *symbols* which have a double nature and are akin to images:

"In a Symbol there is concealment and yet revelation: here, therefore, by Silence and by Speech acting together, comes a double significance. And if both the Speech be itself high, and the Silence fit and noble, how expressive will their union be! Thus in many a painted Device, or simple Seal-emblem, the commonest Truth stands out to us proclaimed with quite new emphasis."

Carlyle even mentions a shoe-image:

"Of Symbols, however, I remark further, that they have both an extrinsic and intrinsic value; oftenest the former only. What, for instance, was in that clouted Shoe, which the Peasants bore aloft with them as ensign in their **Bauernkrieg** *(Peasants' War)?"*

The social function of this ensign was to unify a group of people.

According to Carlyle, there is a deeper significance to symbols, that is, they conceal/reveal the presence of the Almighty:

"In the Symbol proper, what we can call a Symbol, there is ever, more or less distinctly and directly, some embodiment and revelation of the Infinite; the Infinite is made to blend itself with the Finite, to stand visible, and as it were, attainable there. By Symbols, accordingly, is man guided and commanded, made happy, made wretched. He everywhere finds himself encompassed with Symbols, recognised as such or not recognised: the Universe is but one vast Symbol of God; nay, if thou wilt have it, what is man himself but a Symbol of God; "

Again, this way of thinking corresponds closely to Vincent's world view. The above may be summarized as follows: a shoe-image stands for real shoes,which symbolize humanity,which in turn symbolize God.

In the light of the above our search for literary sources could legitimately be extended to the Bible, especially since van Gogh, the son of a preacher and a one-time missionary himself knew it well. Shoes that have become old as the result of a long journey are mentioned in the Bible. The removal of shoes is also mentioned several times with varying symbolic connotations: a sign of reverence; of disgrace; of a contract; and of mourning. Clearly, not all these meanings can be ascribed to the *'Old shoes'* painting. However, one in particular does seem to be relevant: in Ruth, chapter four, an ancient custom of the Israelites is described, namely the exchange of a shoe to indicate the transferance of land ownership from one person to another (only the owner of the land had the right to walk over it). To generalize: van Gogh's painting implies that those who own the shoes are the rightful owners of the earth or ground upon which they stand.

The religious significance of the *'Old shoes'* can easily be confirmed by reference to other works by van Gogh in which natural objects, landscapes and scenes of agricultural labour are infused with a Christian ideology by means of 'hidden' symbolism. For various reasons, the use of overt Christian iconography was, for painters like van Gogh and Millet, inadmissible. By means of metonomy, Realism in their hands became a form of Symbolism. Vincent's Christianity was secularized in that humanity was endowed with God-like attributes. For van Gogh it was the poor and the workers who truly embodied humanity not the rich and the powerful; this is why humanity as a whole can be represented in terms of a pair of down-at-heel shoes.

The question of ownership (2)

An examination of van Gogh's series of Paris shoe paintings reveals that the shoes he painted were ankle-high leather shoes or boots with laces; in one instance there is a pair with elastic sides instead of laces. The shoes are often rough and worn. The more crudely made ones with studs on the soles suggest that they are those of workmen; the more elegant ones suggest that they are for Sunday best or that they belong to clerks or office workers. All the shoes appear to belong to men. In my view what can be claimed with reasonable certainty is that these shoes belonged to male city-dwellers who were members of the petty-bourgeoisie, in all probability a bohemian sub-culture within the petty-bourgeoisie with attachments to the urban proletariat. Hence I would argue that the *'Old shoes'* painting is not so much a personal portrait as that of an individual who belongs to a particular social group. It was a *self*-portrait in so far as Vincent van Gogh was a member of that social group. The fact that Vincent deliberately dirtied the shoes or boots before painting them suggests that he wanted to make a connection with toil, with the workers. Vincent preferred shoes that were old and worn; he wanted shoes that exhibited their history of use. And by contrasting the dark uppers of the shoes against a light ground he endows them with a kind of halo which embodies the saintliness Vincent attributed to work and workers.

Bogomila Welsh-Ovcharov, the author of a detailed study of Vincent's Paris period, argues convincingly that in 1885 Vincent made a conscious decision to shift the focus of his work from the country to the city, from the peasantry to the urban workers, hence his journey first to Antwerp and then to Paris. She comments: *"once living in the Paris suburbs . . . Vincent would have to switch from wearing sabots to the normal boots of the Parisian worker, if he wished to understand and represent the Parisian ambient as effectively as that of Brabant. Eventually Vincent identified so personally with the Parisian working classes that he regularly wore the blue jacket of a zinc worker on his painting expeditions . . . and there can be little doubt that the hob nailed boots which predominate within the five Paris treatments of the shoe subject were his own".*[14]

That Vincent identified his work as an artist with that of other craftsmen, in particular *shoe*-makers, is indicated by his remarks to Theo (letter 626) that painters should work as regularly and be as productive as shoemakers and that he would rather be *"a shoemaker than a musician in colours"* As Derrida explains, Heidegger is on firm ground when he makes a link between shoes as things/products and works of art as things/products because shoes and paintings do have this in common. Even so, the social significance of this identity is overlooked, that is, Vincent's identification of his work as an artist with that of humble artisans such as shoemakers.

Schuh-werke

Another methodological difference between art historians and philosophers is that the former do not limit their study of a work of art to its relationship with its motif, with its real referent, but explore in addition the intramural relationship between it and other imagery of a similar kind. In other words, art historians recognise that artists draw as much from art as they do from life, that there are artistic traditions (iconographic, generic) which often supply artists with their imagery rather than direct perceptions of contemporary reality. Therefore, van Gogh's shoe paintings gain their specific character as signs when considered as links in a whole chain of shoe images which can be traced back at least as far as the *bundschuh* emblems which adorned the banners carried by the German peasants in the war of 1525.

An opportunity to explore this iconographic dimension was provided by the exhibition *Schuh-werke* held at the Nurenberg Kunsthalle in 1976. In an essay in the catalogue of this exhibition, Claus Korte relates van Gogh's shoe pictures firstly to Millet's use of sabots as a personal motto, and secondly to caricatures by Cham of sabot-pictures ridiculing the work of Gustave Courbet.[15] Korte argues that the shoe/sabot motif arose from the battle of the realists against the idealists in the 1850s. He also relates van Gogh's shoe paintings to the history of the still-life genre and points out that in Holland van Gogh painted sabots grouped together with other objects whereas in Paris the shoes were portrayed in isolation. Only in Paris did van Gogh focus exclusively upon the shoes and present them devoid of any context.

The shoes as a cultural sign

Let us now consider what meaning can be derived from direct perception of a pair of shoes. Heidegger often cites utensils, tools, and other equipment as examples in order to make certain philosophical points. As he rightly suggests, our usual attitude to tools is instrumental and functional: normally we are only concerned with their utility and reliability. We can, however, study tools or a pair of shoes in a different light. The shoes belong to someone, they take up the shape of that person's feet, they remind us of the journeys made by the owner and, by extension, the life-journey upon which the owner is engaged, the shoes stand for that person metonymically when the person is absent, hence they can serve as a portrait of that person. To view a pair of shoes in this way is to regard them not as useful tools but as a *sign*. When Heidegger evokes the associations of paths, the life-journey, the toil of the worker, he is perfectly justified in doing so (however, that toil, journey, etc., was not that of a peasant but that of a city dweller). In my view, our perception of the world, even before its rendition in terms of a medium such as painting or photography, is already meaningful or semiotic; 'the world' is a tissue of signs. The question then arises 'what changes take place when a perceptual sign is rendered in terms of a medium to produce a pictorial sign?'.

What we must needs postulate is that certain characteristics of perceptual signs are capable of being translated or carried over into pictorial signs (or alternatively that pictorial signs are capable of reproducing some of the characteristics of the visual display), since if it were otherwise we would not be able to say that a painting of a pair of shoes *resembled* the shoes serving as model. However, since pictures are clearly not identical with what they represent we must also take account of the ways in which pictorial signs *differ* from their referents. Let us list the ways in which perceptual and pictorial signs are similar. In the first place in order to attend to an object the perceiver must select and isolate it from all the other objects in the immediate environment, this act is equivalent to drawing a frame around the object, which is precisely what the artist does literally. In the second place the perceiver adopts a certain viewpoint and angle of vision towards the object which again is what an artist must do in order to draw it. If the artist then renders the object according to the laws of linear perspective the resulting image will exhibit certain features which are comparable to those to be found in the visual display itself. Let us now consider some of the ways in which pictorial signs diverge from their referents. The space of the picture is imaginary and not real hence the three-dimensionality of the depicted objects cannot be explored by means of touch. Scale is often different: the painted shoes may be larger or smaller than the real shoes. Their material is clearly different: the real shoes are made of leather while all depicted items consist of pigment (the way the pigment is applied may simulate the appearance of leather or it may not). All in all there is a marked reduction of visual information in pictorial signs compared to direct perception.

However difficult it may be for theorists to explain iconic signs there is no doubt that human beings find it a simple matter to see painted lines and patterns as shoes or faces or trees while knowing perfectly well *at the same time* that they are viewing painted marks on a flat surface. Our conviction that we can see shoes even when we are also aware of the thick brushstrokes of paint which constitute the shoe-image – in van Gogh's case the work of artistic production is strongly foregrounded – is unshakeable. It is my contention, therefore, that the painter fixes and heightens perceptual signs via the medium of oil painting simultaneously reproducing and transforming those perceptual signs. Hence, it is legitimate for a critic to treat an image of shoes as if it conveyed the same meaning as a pair of real shoes considered as a sign, but the critic then needs to go further and consider the additional factors of the medium itself and the way (style) in which the shoes have been painted.

As already mentioned, van Gogh always foregrounds his means of production – pigments, brushmarks – so that the work of picture-making is made visible; (the *'Old shoes'* painting exhibits the history of its production in the same way that the old shoes themselves exhibit the history of their use). Thus his representational paintings call attention to the fact that they are different from what they represent even as they represent it. In this respect van Gogh complies with Adorno's aphorism *"Language becomes a measure of truth only when we are conscious of the non-identity of an expression with what we mean".*[16] (In the terminology of semiotics: a sign in which the difference between signifier and signified is strongly marked.)

A double paradox governs the *'Old shoes'* picture: the real shoes are absent from the picture but at the same time present via their pictorial representation; the owner of the shoes is absent from the picture but at the same time present via the shoes which serve as a surrogate for the owner.

Derrida's position on the question of ownership is that this matter can never be settled definitively because the actual owner is always literally absent from the painting. (He also observes that *painted* shoes cannot belong to anyone.) One might add that since shoes can be exchanged it is possible for them to be owned by several people in succession. And since shoes are normally manufactured in 'editions' the same type of shoe can be owned by hundreds of people simultaneously. Let us acknowledge that the question of ownership cannot be resolved with absolute finality, nevertheless, the various interpretations of the van Gogh and ascriptions of ownership of the shoes forwarded since 1886 can surely be grounded in the social and historical circumstances in which, firstly, the picture was produced, and secondly, in which the interpretations were produced.

Van Gogh's peasant style

It is at this point that the French defenders of Heidegger are able to mount a counter-attack upon Schapiro. Van Gogh, they correctly point out, set himself the task of becoming a peasant painter. They then go on to argue that his bold, vigorous style of painting and artisanal practice embodied a peasant ideology, therefore Heidegger's response to the *'Old shoes'* picture was valid because he intuitively grasped the peasant ideology of the picture's style even if he made an error about the ownership of the shoes themselves. It is certainly true that Vincent felt himself to be 'a dog with dirty paws' in polite society and that his crude manner of painting was part of a conscious strategy of representing the values of the unpolished lower classes – peasants and workers – in a bourgeois milieu, and also the simple values of Nature and rural life in the midst of over-sophisticated city life.[17] This peasant-and-poor-workers ideology, was not, however, the ideology of actual peasants or workers, it was an ideology attributed to the peasantry by an artist–intellectual who by birth, education and profession was a member of the petty-bourgeoisie. Such peasant ideologies may be true or false, progressive or reactionary. In Heidegger's case his peasant ideology was uncomfortably close to that promoted by the Nazis. Heidegger shows no awareness of the humanitarian impulse which caused Vincent to identify with the exploited, he shows no interest in the problems faced by actual peasants in the second half of the nineteenth century or in the 1930s. And despite the ingenious arguments forwarded by his defenders, he shows no interest in the way in which the *'Old shoes'* picture is painted or in van Gogh's ambitions to be a peasant painter like his hero Millet.

Heidegger and Nazism

Critical opinion is sharply divided as to the merits of Heidegger's philosophy. His work provokes extreme reactions both for and against. His writings are notoriously convoluted and obscure. George Steiner summarizes the anti-Heidegger case as follows: *"His writings are a thicket of impenetrable verbiage; the questions he poses are sham-questions; the doctrines he puts forward are, so far as anything at all can be made of them, either false or trivial . . . the nebulous vortex of his rhetoric is nothing less than disaster-*

ous, both philosophically and politically".[18] On the other hand, Heidegger cannot be ignored because his ideas have been so influential on so many intellectuals, especially in France. Since I am not a professional philosopher I am not really qualified to comment upon Heidegger's work but I must acknowledge a prejudice against it. The question of Being which so preoccupied Heidegger seems to me a silly, vacuous issue to address. (Compare Marx: his object of analysis was Capital, his purpose was to change the world not to interpret it.) In so far as I can follow Adorno's scathing critique of Heidegger in *Negative dialectics* I agree with it.[19] Above all, what justifies a sceptical approach to Heidegger is the fact that the only time in his life when he took any notice of politics and the society of which he was a member he supported the Nazis. In 1933 he wrote: *"Let not doctrines and 'Ideas' be the rule of your being. Today and in the future, only the Führer himself is German reality and its law".* Heidegger's enthusiasm for the Nazis only lasted nine months but as Steiner puts it: *"Is there anywhere in Heidegger's work a repudiation of Nazism, is there anywhere, from 1945 to his death (in 1976), a single syllable on the realities, on the philosophical implications of the world of Auschwitz? These are the questions that count. And the answer would have to be, No".*[20]

Steiner goes on to find disturbing parallels between the language of *Being and time* and the jargon of Nazism; Heidegger's language, he claims, *"fits effortlessly into the Nazi cult of 'blood and soil' ".* Heidegger had a cottage built at Todtnauberg in the Black forest in 1922 and lived there for many months each year writing his philosophy in solitude. His texts abound with references to forests, woodcutter's paths, and to clearings. During the period 1930 to 1935 when Heidegger wrote *'The origin of the work of art'* in which he refers so many times to peasant experience and to the earth, the Nazi racial theorists were spreading their evil blood and soil doctrines and glorifying the German peasantry as the true source of the Aryan master race. Was it merely co-incidence that Heidegger's philosophy should have resembled these Nazi doctrines so closely? Heidegger was born in 1889 in Messkirch in the Black Forest region of Baden-Wurtenberg. His father was the sexton of a Catholic church. Heidegger spent his life as a university teacher and intellectual.[21] He was, therefore, in class terms a member of the petty-bourgeoisie. Why then did Heidegger misrecognise a pair of shoes belonging to a member of his own class as those of a peasant unless that misrecognition was a symptom of the Nazi ideology which hailed the coming of a simple man, 'a peasant as it were', who would solve all problems, that is, Adolf Hitler.[22]

The truth of the work of art according to Heidegger

Let us try to be scrupulously fair to Heidegger. What in his view is the truth of the *'Old shoes'* painting? According to Heidegger what the work of art does is to disclose the essential nature of shoes as equipment. Their essential nature is described in his remark: *"The art work lets us know what shoes are in truth . . . the equipmentality of equipment first genuinely arrives at its appearance through the work and only in the work".* He rejects the idea of a copy-relation between real shoes and an image of shoes: *"the work, therefore, is not the reproduction of some particular entity that happens to be present at any given time; it is, on the contrary, the reproduction of the thing's general essence".* What is at work in the work of art is *"the disclosure of the particular being in its being, the happening of truth . . . The art work opens up in its own way the Being of beings. This opening up, i.e. this deconcealing, i.e. the truth of beings, happens in the work. In the artwork, the truth of what is has set itself to work. Art is truth setting itself to work".*[23]

If van Gogh were alive today he would be most surprised to find that according to Heidegger no copy-relation existed between the shoes and the painting, because van Gogh spent years copying: he copied from plaster casts, from the figure,

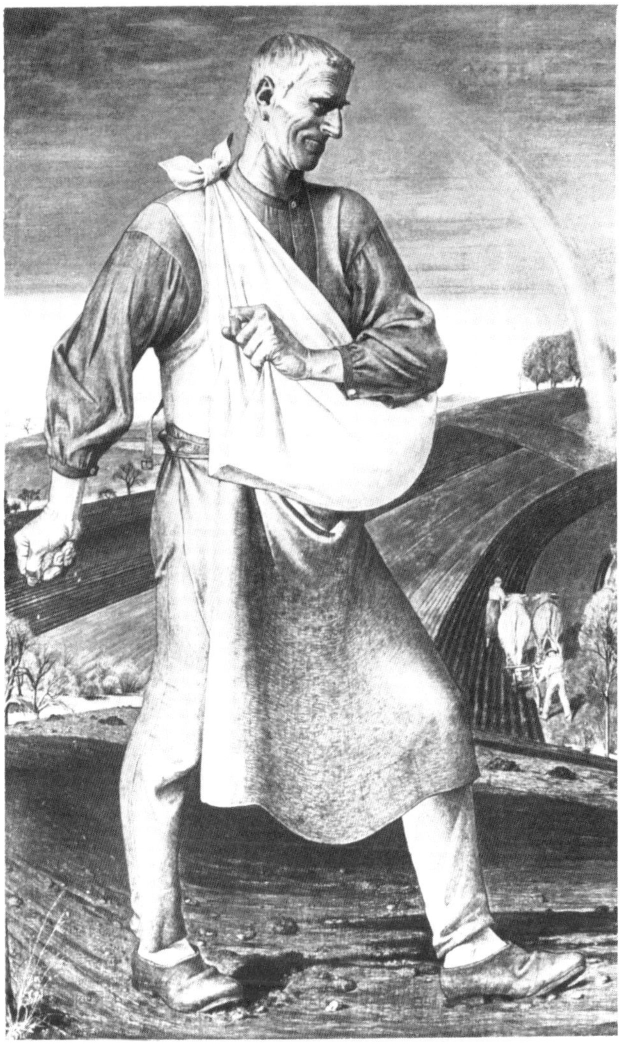

(83) Oskar Martin-Amorbach, *The sower,* 1937, oil on board, 253.5 x 163 cm, Property of the Federal Republic of Germany.

from Nature, from illustrations and prints in order to improve his drawing; he was one of the most assiduous copyists in the whole history of art![24] Furthermore, van Gogh was most reluctant to work without a model, to work from his imagination. There was no need, he believed, to depict Biblical events which he had not personally witnessed in order to convey a religious sentiment because if God existed his presence would be manifest throughout Nature. He also believed that such feelings could be communicated via contrasts of complementary colours. It is clear from van Gogh's paintings and letters that everyday objects such as chairs and shoes were charged with symbolic meanings and that his aim as a painter was to communicate those meanings. In sharp contrast to Heidegger, van Gogh was always concerned with the concrete and particular. It was not an essence of shoes -'shoeness'- he was after but a depiction of this particular pair of shoes; the chair which I use, the chair which Gauguin uses. And because van Gogh was so committed to the actual and concrete, his shoes are indubitably those of a particular kind, historical era, and social class.

Meyer Schapiro has the reputation of being a Marxist art historian (if he is he disguises it quite well because one of his ex-students has claimed that he never realised at the time that he was being taught by a Marxist).[25] We should expect, therefore, to find in his critique of Heidegger evidence of an alternative, materialist approach to the van Gogh painting. Yet what we find is the usual psycho-biographical conception of art – the shoes painting is a personal expression, a self-portrait – so prevalent in the literature on van Gogh. Since Marxists believe that we live in the era of capitalism and that this society is divided into antagonistic classes, any Marxist art history ought to place the work of art in that social context and show its relation to the struggle between the classes. In order, therefore, to specify the meaning of the *'Old shoes'* painting with greater precision it would be necessary to investigate the state of the social classes in Paris in 1886. Such historical research could help us to understand the social comment which van Gogh was making about the conditions which he found during his stay in Paris.

Similarly, when we examine the reception of the *'Old shoes'* painting in the 1930s, its appropriation by the philosopher Heidegger, we need to explore the socio-political aspects of that conjuncture – as I have attempted to do briefly here – in which that interpretation was produced.

It has not been my aim to argue that the van Gogh painting has only one meaning because I recognise the fact that images may have multiple meanings, nor to argue that its original 1886 meaning is the only true meaning because I realize that pictorial meaning can change according to social context and through time. Nevertheless, I would maintain that it is possible to distinguish between dominant and subordinate meanings and between accurate and inaccurate readings of images. As long as the painting survives it exists in a series of presents each of which is further away in time from its moment of production. It is not a question of privileging the present interpretation over the past interpretation, or vice versa; it is a question of recognising the persistence of the past in the present and at the same time the difference between now and then. Vincent's painting is at once a part of our contemporary world and simultaneously a relic of an era which has passed. It can still speak to us because we still wear shoes, and the kind of shoes worn is still an index of class belonging.

What this study has highlighted, then, is the basic difference between philosophy and art history, namely, the fact that philosophy is not an *historical* discipline; neither Heidegger nor Derrida attempt to explain Vincent's painting by recourse to history. For the art historian, questions of truth and interpretation can be settled with a reasonable degree of certainty by situating the production and consumption of artistic signs socially and historically. It is this ground which saves the art historian from the philosopher's fantasy world of metaphysical speculation.

Notes and references:

1. Most of the texts on reception history/theory are in German. There are however some summarizing articles in English: David Bathrick 'The politics of reception theory in the GDR' *Minnesota Review* (5) Fall 1975 pp 125–33; P.U. Hohendahl 'Introduction to reception aesthetics' *New German critique* (10) Winter 1977 pp 29–63; H. J. Schmidt 'Reception theory and its applications' *New German Critique* (17) Spring 1979 pp 157–69.

2. M. Heidegger 'The origin of the work of art' *Poetry, Language and thought* (NY: Harper & Row, 1971) pp 15–87.

3. M. Schapiro 'The still-life as personal object – a note on Heidegger and van Gogh' *The reach of mind: essays in memory of Kurt Goldstein 1878–1965*; ed by M. L. Simmel (NY: Springer, 1968) pp 203–9.

4. 'Peinture et philosphie (1) Martin Heidegger et les souliers de van Gogh' *Macula* (3/4) 1978 pp 2–37; J. Derrida 'Restitutions de la vérité en pointure' pp 11–37. See also J. Derrida *La vérité en peinture* (Paris: Flammarion, 1978) to be issued in a translation by the University of Chicago Press.

5. P. Taguiev 'Philosophie et peinture' *Opus international* (72) Spring 1979 pp 48–57.

6. Op cit (2) pp 33–34.

7. Op cit (2) p 40.

8. L. Lowenthal 'The sociology of literature' *Communications in modern society*; ed by W. Schramm (Urbana: University of Illinois Press, 1949) pp 82–100.

9. H. R. Graetz *The symbolic language of Vincent van Gogh* (Thames & Hudson, 1963) pp 46–9.

10. Predictably, Derrida introduces another psychological dimension namely the Freudian psycho-analytic interpretation of shoes as sexual symbols, even though in this case the Freudian connection appears to be entirely spurious. Derrida's reference to it is simply the obligatory ritual gesture of an intellectual operating in a milieu in which Freud and Lacan are dominant figures.

11. F. Gauzi 'Vincent van Gogh (1886–87)' *Van Gogh in perspective*; ed by B. Welsh-Ovcharov (Englewood Cliffs, NJ: Prentice-Hall, 1974) pp 33–34.

12. V. van Gogh *The complete letters* 3 vols (Thames & Hudson, 1958).

13. T. Carlyle *Sartor Resartus* [1833–34] (Collins, n.d.) pp 213–17, 194–7.

14. B. Welsh-Ovcharov *Vincent van Gogh, his Paris period 1886–1888* (Utrecht-Den Haag: Editions Victorine, 1976) p 139.

15. C. Korte 'Van Gogh und das schuh-stilleben der bataille du Réalisme' *Schuhwerke: aspekte zum menschenbild* (Nurenberg: Kunsthalle, 1976) pp 8–16.

16. Adorno,quoted in,*The melancholy science: an introduction to the thought of Theodor W. Adorno* by G. Rose (MacMillan, 1978) p 74.

17. See my article 'Van Gogh as a peasant painter' *Artery* (17) December 1979 pp 14–25.

18. G. Steiner *Heidegger* (Fontana/Collins, 1978) p 12.

19. T. W. Adorno *Negative dialectics* (Routledge & Kegan Paul, 1973) pp 97–131.

20. Op cit (17) p 116.

21. For biographical details of Heidegger see *Martin Heidegger: an illustrated study* by W. Biemel (NY: Harcourt Brace Jovanovich, 1976). For a detailed examination of Heidegger and his connection with Nazism see: S. E. Bronner 'Martin Heidegger: the consequences of political mystification' *Salmagundi* (38–39) Summer–Fall 1977 pp 153–74.

22. Evidence for this contention is cited in my unpublished lecture 'Total Kultur: Nazi art'.

23. Op cit (2) pp 35–9.

24. see C. Chetham *The role of Vincent van Gogh's copies in the development of his art* (NY: Garland, 1978).

25. Wayne Andersen page 68 of *Social research* 45 (1) Spring 1978, special issue on the work of Meyer Schapiro.

Additional bibliography

Readers may be interested in the following recently published articles and books on van Gogh.

Wylie, A.S. 'An investigation of the vocabulary of line in Vincent van Gogh's expression of space' *Oud Holland* 85 (4) 1970 pp 210-38.

Faille, J.B. de la *The works of Vincent van Gogh: his paintings and drawings* (Weidenfeld & Nicolson, rev. ed. 1970).

Heelan, P.A. 'Toward a new analysis of the pictorial space of Vincent van Gogh' *Art Bulletin* 54 (4) Dec 1972 pp 478-92.

Les sources d'inspiration de Vincent van Gogh (Paris: Institut Neerlandais, 1972).

Prados, M. 'Vincent van Gogh's childhood and boyhood: a psychoanalytical inquiry' *The human context* 6 (1) 1974 pp 194-213.

Mauron, C. *Van Gogh: études psychocritiques* (Paris: Corti, 1976).

Ward, J. L. 'A re-examination of van Gogh's pictorial space' *Art Bulletin* 58 (4) Dec 1976 pp 593-604.

Pollock, G. & Orton, F. *Vincent van Gogh: artist of his time* (Phaidon, 1978).

Johnson, R. 'Vincent van Gogh and the vernacular: his Southern accent' Part I *Arts magazine* 52 (10) June 1978 pp 131-5; Part II *Arts Magazine* 53 (6) Feb 1979 pp 98-104.

Japanese prints collected by Vincent van Gogh (Amsterdam: Rijksmuseum Vincent van Gogh, 1978).

Uitert, E. van *Van Gogh drawings* (Thames & Hudson, 1979).

Hulsker, J. *Van Gogh: the complete works in chronological order* (Phaidon, 1980).

Pollock, G. 'Artists mythologies and media genius, madness and art history' *Screen* 21 (3) 1980 pp 57-96.

Murray, A.H. 'Strange and subtle perspective: van Gogh, the Hague school and the Dutch landscape tradition' *Art history* 3 (4) Dec 1980 pp 410-24.

Zemel, C.M. *The formation of a legend: van Gogh criticism 1890-1920* (Bowker, 1981).

Vincent van Gogh during his Dutch years: urban and rural life as depicted by van Gogh and his contemporaries (Amsterdam: Rijksmuseum Vincent van Gogh, 1981).

Acknowledgements

My thanks to all those museums, private collectors and publishers who supplied photographs of the works reproduced and who granted permission for those works/photographs to be reproduced.

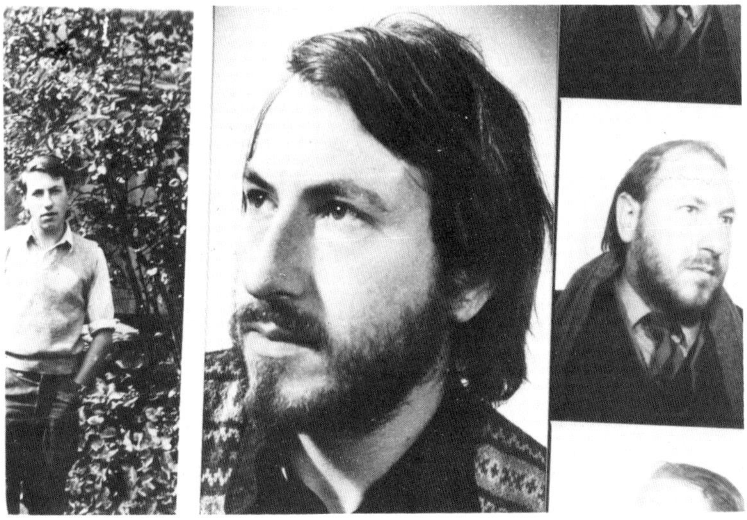

John A. Walker was born in 1938 in Grimsby, Lincolnshire, and trained as a painter at Kings College, Newcastle-upon-Tyne. He has worked in the civil service and in libraries. Currently he lectures in the history and theory of art and design at Middlesex Polytechnic and West Surrey College of Art. He is the author of ***Art since Pop*** **(Thames & Hudson, 1975) and** ***A glossary of art, architecture and design since 1945*** **(Bingley, 2nd ed 1977), and numerous articles in a variety of art periodicals.**